Inspired
to bead

a collection of
necklaces and bracelets

by Stephanie Burnham

Author acknowledgements

*All my love and thanks go to Grant, Sam and Josh for supporting me
with my Bead Studio, designing and writing over the years
and to all my lovely students for their encouragement and friendship
and to Deborah Wood for making my book a reality.*

Published by Stephanie Burnham Publishing
Wakefield Country Courtyard, Wakefield Lodge Estate, Potterspury, Northamptonshire NN12 7QX

Text © Stephanie Burnham
Bead illustrations © Deborah Wood

ISBN: 978-0-9926662-0-0

www.thebeadscene.com

Contents

The designs included in this book stem from over fifteen years of designing and teaching beadwork. Many of my students have been on this journey with me, never minding what I threw at them next and always ready for a challenge.

As you look through the designs you will see that I have a great love of colour and texture, using a variety of sizes and shapes to achieve many different looks.

Many of the designs can be customised to suit your own personal taste. Don't be afraid to venture off the beaten track, this is usually when wonderfully creative things happen.

All the major stitches are featured and explained in full, or referenced back to another project within the book.

I do hope you enjoy working through the designs and – as I say to my students – it's the first two rows that are the trickiest!

Happy beading,

Stephanie

all square bracelet

beads you need

- 10g 4mm cube beads
- 10g size 8 seed beads
- 10g 5mm bugle beads
- Beading needle and thread
- 2-bar clasp

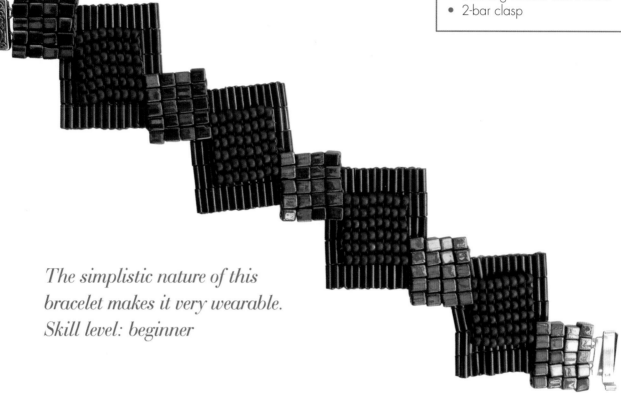

The simplistic nature of this bracelet makes it very wearable.
Skill level: beginner

1 The technique used for this bracelet is *square stitch*. The bracelet is made up using a series of squares. There are **5 squares of 4mm cubes** in the original bracelet, if you require a longer length you just need to add more squares.

2 Thread up using **1 metre** of beading thread, pick up **1x 4mm cube bead**, pass it down to within 20cm from the tail end of the thread and then pass the needle back through the cube to secure, creating a 'stop' bead.

3 Thread on **3 more cubes**, pick up a **4th cube**, pass the needle back through the **4th cube** on the initial row (threading away from yourself), thread back through the cube you have just added threading back towards yourself.

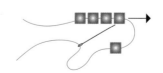

4 Pick up another cube, thread back through the **3rd cube** of the initial row and pass the needle through the cube you have just added. Add **2 further cubes** in the same way to complete the second row.

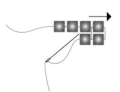

5 To secure the first two rows, run the thread back through the initial row then through the row you have just created. This is also a good time to remove the loop from around the stop bead as it is no longer needed.

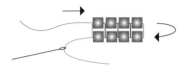

6 **5 rows** are needed for each square. Continue to add rows until you have **5 in total**, remembering that after each row is completed you need to thread back though the previous and the row just added for extra strength.

7 When the first square is completed, bring the needle out of the second row along at one end. Thread on **8x size 8 seed beads**, work the second row in square stitch as before whilst keeping the beads as close to the square of cubes as possible.

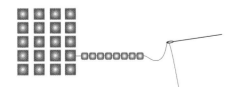

8 As you bead back towards the cube square and finish the second row of **size 8 seed beads**, thread back through both rows as usual and pass the needle back into the cube square to make a secure join. This can be done a couple of times for extra strength.

9 The **size 8 bead square** consists of **6 rows**. Work **alternate** squares of **size 8 seed beads** and **4mm cubes**, making sure that the joins are as secure as possible. Make the row of squares long enough to fit your wrist.

10 Each **size 8 bead** square has a **bugle bead square** behind it. This is also *square stitch* using **5x bugle beads** across and **14x rows long**.

The squares are then *stab-stitched* on to the back of the size 8 squares. Centre the squares over each other as much as possible.

11 Before adding the clasp you may wish to reinforce the cube square on to the edges of the bugle squares for added strength. There is no technique to this, simply move up and down, in and out, through both the beads and squares to secure.

12 Finally, add the two-bar clasp by fixing it through the **second** and **fourth** cube along on each of the ends. Pass through the cubes and fixing points of the clasp several times to secure.

DESIGNER TIP

If you find that an extra square will give you too much length, just make a half or three-quarter square.

boho bubbles bracelet

bracelet

beads you need

- Selection of size 10, 8 and 6 pearl beads in three colours
- 10g size 11 seed beads in toning colour
- 1 toggle clasp
- 1 large heart
- Beading needle and thread

Lots of texture to play with in this bracelet. Try experimenting with different sizes of pearls. Skill level: beginner

1 Cut a length of beading thread **1.5m**; thread both ends of the thread through the eye of the needle creating a loop at the base.

2 Pass the needle through the **fixing point** on one half of the **toggle clasp**, then pass the needle through the loop at the base of the thread and pull up firmly, this anchors the thread to the fixing point of the toggle.

6 **Three** to **four** pearls are added in between each pearl on the base row, these are best varied in size as they will 'nestle' better together.

3 Thread on **5 seed beads** followed by a **10mm pearl**, repeat until the bracelet is the correct length.

4 When the last pearl is added, thread on **5 further seed beads**, pass the needle through the fixing point of the **second half** of the **toggle clasp**.

7 Continue to add **pearls** until the bracelet is completed, the **heart** is added separately in the centre of the necklace using a **circle of seed beads** and you may find you only need a **couple of pearls** in that section to allow the heart to move freely.

5 Working now with **one** thread (the other can be used when the initial thread is finished), pass the needle through the **first** seed bead of this section then **thread on a pearl** and seed bead, pass the needle back **down** through the **pearl** missing out the seed bead and into the **next seed bead** along.

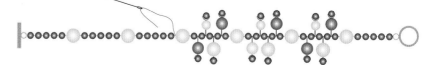

necklace

beads you need

- 8mm pearls in two colours
  main colour 30, contrast 20
- 5g size 6, 8 and 11 seed beads
  in two colours
- S-lon beading thread
- Beading needle
- 2m organza ribbon

This necklace is a
great introduction to
right angle weave.
Skill level: intermediate

1 ROW 1: Starting with one colour way, thread on **1x 8m pearl** and **1x size 11 seed bead**, repeat until you have **5x 8mm pearls** added. Pass the needle back through all

the beads just added from the tail end of the thread and secure the beads into a circle with a double knot.

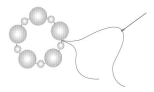

2 ROW 2: Pass the needle through the first pearl again, pick up **2x size 8 seed beads**, pass the needle through the **second pearl along**, continue until there are **2x size 8 seed beads** sitting above each of the **size 11 seed beads** in row one, pass through the **first pearl** once again.

3 ROW 3: Pass the needle through the first **size 8 seed bead** of the first pair, add **1x size 6 seed bead**, pass the needle through the second of the **size 8 beads**.

4 Continue threading through the beads whilst adding **1x size 6 seed bead** between each 'pair' of **size 8 seed beads**.

5 ROW 4: Pass the needle through the beads until you have threaded through a **size 6 seed bead**, pick up **1x size 8 seed bead**, **1x size 11 seed bead**, **1x 8mm pearl**, **1x size 11** and **1x size 8 seed bead**. Pass the needle through the next **size 6** along, repeat until you have four more **8mm pearls** added. This makes the first 'cluster'.

6 Pull on the thread as you work so that it gives a raised effect to your 'cluster' and as the pearls are fairly large it will help to keep the tension firm. It is a good idea to thread around the 'cluster' one more time and pull tightly and then tie off with a double knot.

7 Make four further 'clusters' in the same way making **three** in the first colourway and **two** in the second colourway.

8 These 'clusters' are strung together using **size 11 seed beads** to join the 'flat' sides (see photo). Thread on and join **5x size 11 seed beads** at the top and **3x size 11 seed beads** at the bottom.

9 ADDING THE RIBBON:
Cut the **2m** length in half, fold one piece in half again and pass the folded end of the ribbon through the side edge of the end 'cluster' then pass the two ends of the ribbon through the folded loop. Repeat on the other side.

pansy bracelet

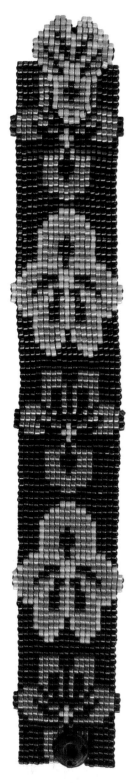

This bracelet is so pretty and can be customised to your favourite pansy shades. Skill level: beginner

beads you need

- **FOR THE YELLOW PANSIES:**
  5g size 11 cylinder beads in **bright yellow, light yellow, green** *(as used in background)*, **cream** for centre of pansy *(a few)*

- **FOR PURPLE PANSIES:**
  5g size 11 cylinder beads in **dark purple, medium purple, light purple, bright yellow** and **white** for centre of pansy *(a few)*

- Long and short beading needles
- KO/Nymo beading thread
- Press slud
- Note pad, pencil, rubber *(to mark your chart off)*

1 Firstly, empty a small amount of **all** colours to be used on to your beading mat. Thread a beading needle with **1m** of beading thread.

2 **STARTING TO SQUARE STITCH:** Place the bracelet pattern next to you and note the starting arrow on the grid. Then, working from left to right, thread on the **first colour bead** down to about **10cm** from the tail end of the thread. Pass the needle back up through the bead creating a **'stop' bead**.

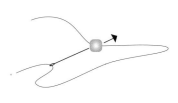

3 Continue to thread on this entire row of beads, there should be **19 beads** in total including the 'stop' bead.

4 Thread the **first bead** of the **second row** on to your thread, and position the bead so that it sits directly underneath the **last right hand bead** of the **first row**.

5 Pass the needle back through the **last bead** of the **first row**, then turn the needle passing back through the **first bead** of the **second row** just added. Continue along the row adding beads in exactly the same way, being careful to note the colour changes as you work.

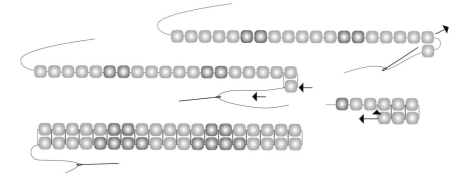

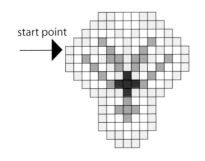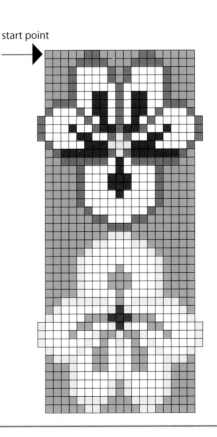

6 When the second row is complete, pass the needle back through the **initial row** of beads added, then thread through the **second row** once again. Threading through the two rows of beads gives extra stability to the beads and brings them nicely into line.

8 SQUARE STITCH – INCREASING ON THE OUTSIDE EDGES:
To increase on either of the outside edges, bring the needle through the last bead on the row you wish to increase. Thread on one more bead, plus the first bead of the next row.

Thread back through the increase bead.

7 Continue to add rows in the same manner until you reach the point at which the pansy petals extend beyond the outer edge of the bracelet.

9 Thread through the first bead of the next row and continue along in the usual way. You can add as many beads as you wish for an increase, just square stitch your way back into the main section of the beadwork to secure.

When the increases are in place you will return to the normal size of the cuff. Continue working each row as the pattern states remembering to place the pansies petal to petal. The original bracelet has five base pansies in total but you may find you need slightly more or less, just stop the design when the cuff-ends butt up to each other.

PATTERN FOR PANSY BRACELET

PURPLE PANSY
- Dark purple [DB 004]
- Medium purple [DB 047]
- Light purple [DB 249]
- Bright yellow [DB 160]
- White [DB 202]

YELLOW PANSY
- Bright yellow [DB 160]
- Light yellow
- Green [DB 011]
- Cream [DB 203]

SMALL PANSY
- Bright yellow [DB 160]
- Light yellow
- Green [DB 011]
- Cream [DB203]

start point

start point

10 CREATING THE SMALLER PANSY:

This is done by decreasing in *square stitch*. Start at the first of the three longest rows towards the centre of the pansy, when these are complete you will need to work a decrease as follows:

SQUARE STITCH – DECREASING:

When the previous row is finished prior to the decreasing row, run the threads through as usual, firstly through the row above then, through the row you have just completed, but instead of the running the thread through the entire row, bring the needle out of the bead you wish to start the next decreased row.

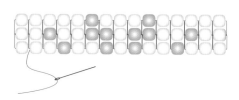

Thread on a bead and go back through the bead the thread is coming out of, then go back through the bead just added.

Continue along the row until you reach the bead where you wish to start the next row. Add the first bead of the next row and continue as usual. Continue working the pansy, first on one side then the other to finish.

start point
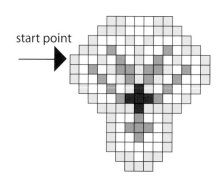

CONSTRUCTING THE CUFF BRACELET:

11

The smaller pansy needs to be stab-stitched into place on one end of the cuff with approximately half the pansy extending beyond one end of the cuff.

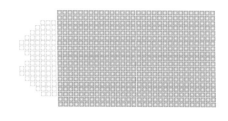

12

A press-stud is then stab-stitched into place, one half on the other end of the cuff, the other on the underside of the smaller pansy which is extending off the other end of the cuff.

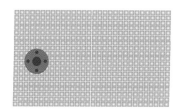
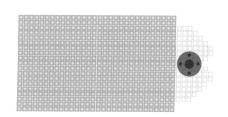

bracelet

beads you need

- 9-10x 10mm pearls
- 8-9x 9mm pearls
- 5g size 11 seed beads in two colours
- Beading needle and thread
- Lobster clasp and split ring

A great project to kick start your beading journey.
Skill level: beginner

1 Using **1.5m** thread, pick up **1x 10mm pearl** and pass it down to within **15cm** of the tail end of your thread.

2 Pick up **11x size 11 seed beads**, pass the needle back through the pearl once again 'wrapping' it with the beads.

3 Repeat until you have **six** wraps around this initial pearl.

4 Thread on **1x 9mm pearl** followed by a **10mm pearl**. This second pearl needs to be wrapped in exactly the same way as the first pearl. Six wraps around each in total.

5 Continue adding and wrapping pearls in the same way until the bracelet reaches the desired length.

6 When you reach the end add the clasp at this point in the usual way. On the return journey the **9mm pearls** need to be wrapped. This is done in exactly the same way as before, only this time **6x size 11 seed beads** are used on each wrap, with a total of **10 wraps** around each **9mm pearl**, passing through each **10mm pearl** as you work.

7 When you reach the end of the bracelet add the other part of the clasp before finishing the thread, making sure you double knot your thread for extra security.

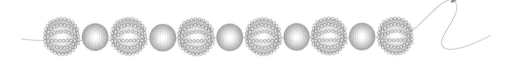

DESIGNER TIP

Remember to keep the second 10mm pearl 'tight' as you wrap so there is just a small gap between pearls.

sweet pea lattice bracelet

bracelet

beads you need

- 10g size 11 seed beads in three toning colours tone 1 ⚬, tone 2 ⚬, tone 3 ⚬
- 49 x 4mm crystals
- 1 x 6mm pearl (for clasp)
- Beading needle and thread

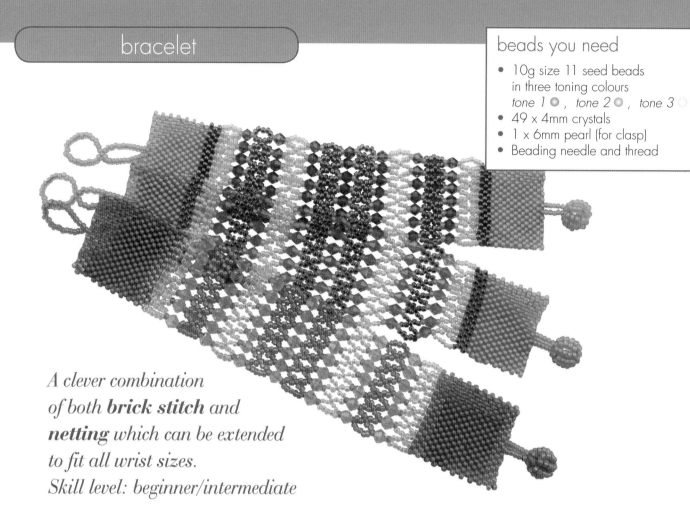

*A clever combination of both **brick stitch** and **netting** which can be extended to fit all wrist sizes.*
Skill level: beginner/intermediate

1 The two bases at both ends of the cuff are worked separately, in your chosen main colour *(tone 1 ⚬)* of **size 11 seed beads**.

ROW 1: Start by creating a **14 bead ladder** for the initial row. Thread **1m** beading thread, pick up **two size 11 seed beads**, pass them down to within **20cm** of the tail end of your thread, pass the needle back through

first bead added pulling on the thread so that the two beads sit side by side. Pass the needle back down through the **second** bead along again.

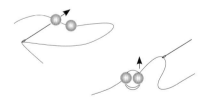

Pick up a **third** bead, pass the needle back up through the **second** bead then back down through the bead just added. Continue adding beads until you have a total of **14** in a row.

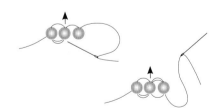

2 **ROW 2:** Pick up **2x size 11 seed beads**, pass the needle through the **second** loop of the **first row** then thread the needle up through the **first** bead, down through the

second, through the **second** loop once again then up through the **second** bead. This is called the *locking stitch*. By adding two beads at the start of each row

it stops there being a thread around the side of the first bead; it also stops the initial bead from leaning inwards.

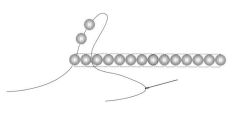
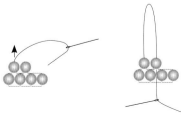

3 Pick up a **third** bead, pass the needle through the **third** loop along on top of the **first row**, then thread back up through the bead just added. Continue to add beads in the same way until you reach the end of row. This technique is known as *brick stitch*.

You will notice that on the second row the end beads are slightly set in from the first, this is quite normal and is correct.

4 **ROW 3:** Pick up **two seed beads**, pass the needle through the **first** loop of the **second row**, pass the needle back up through the **first** of the beads just added, then down through the **second**, through the loop then back up through the **second** bead. This movement makes the bead stick proud of the **first bead** of the **second row** and is correct.

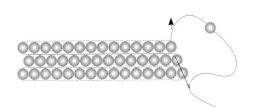

5 Continue in the same manner until you reach the **last bead** which has to be added, as you would for a *square stitch* bead to complete the pattern so that the last bead is slightly sticking out over the last bead of the second row. **14** rows are needed in total for each cuff base. Work **three more rows** in a second colour *(tone 2 ◐)*, making **17 rows** in total.

NOTE:-
The first of the three rows contains **14** beads, second **13** beads and the third **14** beads.

THE CENTRAL NETTING:

6 Place both beaded bases on to a beading mat; bring your working thread through the **first** bead of the **second** colour *(tone 2 ◐)* at the side of **one** block of beadwork.

ROW 1: Thread on 5x *tone 3* ○ , 1x *tone 1* ◐, 1x crystal, 1x *tone 1* ◐, 5x *tone 2* ◐, 1x *tone 1* ◐, 1x crystal, 1x *tone 1* ◐, 5x *tone 3* ○ , 1x *tone 1* ◐, 1x crystal, 1x *tone 1* ◐, 5x *tone 2* ◐, 1x *tone 1* ◐, 1x crystal, 1x *tone 1* ◐, 5x *tone 2* ◐, 1x *tone 1* ◐, 1x crystal, 1x *tone 1* ◐, 5x *tone 3* ○ , 1 x *tone 1* ◐, 1x crystal, 1x *tone 1* ◐, 5x *tone 3* ○ , 1x *tone 1* ◐, 1x crystal, 1x *tone 1* ◐, 5x *tone 3* ○ then pass the needle through the corresponding bead on the other half of the beaded square. (See Fig.1)

Fig.1

7 **ROW 2:** Thread on 5x *tone 3* ○, pass the needle through the *tone 1* ◐, crystal bead and *tone 1* ◐ of the initial row. Thread on 5x *tone 2* ◐, pass the needle through the *tone 1* ◐, crystal bead and *tone 1* ◐ of the first row. Continue in the same manner until the second row of netting is complete.

bracelet

DESIGNER TIP

You can at this stage, before you add the bead and loop fasteners, add three extra rows on to each end of the brick stitch bracelet base if you wish. This will give you a little extra length and add another twist to the design.

THE CENTRAL NETTING (cont'd):

8 Pass the needle through the **second** bead along on the base of the netting and up through the **third** bead along. (See Fig.2)

Fig.2

9 **ROW 3:** Pick up 2x *tone 3* ○ seed beads; pass the needle through the **third** bead of the previous row, pick up two more *tone 3* ○ seed beads, 1x *tone 1* ◉, 1 crystal bead,

1x *tone 1* ◉ and 2x tone 2 ◉ seed beads, pass the needle through the **third** bead of the loop in the previous row. (See Fig. 3) Continue to work along the row changing colours as you need

to. When you reach the other side, pass the needle through the **third** bead along on the block of beads, then up through the **fourth** bead along to begin the **fourth** row.

Fig.3

10 **ROW 4:** Repeat rows 1 to 3 to continue adding rows until the netting is complete. (See Fig.4)

Fig.4

BEAD & LOOP FASTENER:

11 Pass the needle out through the **seventh** bead on the outside edge of one side of the block of beading, thread on **6x tone 1 ◎ seed beads, 1x 6mm pearl**, pick up a further **6x tone 1 ◎ seed beads**, and pass the needle back **up through the pearl**, thread on

6 more tone 1 ◎ seed beads, pass the needle back **up through the pearl**. Pass the needle **down** through one of the **6** sets of beads on the **outside** of the pearl and pass the needle through the **last** of the **first 6 beads added**. Pick up **5x tone 1 ◎ seed beads** and

pass the needle **down** through the **eighth** bead on the block of beading. Continue to journey up and around the pearl which will do two things; it will cover the pearl and give strength to the clasp stalk. Double knot to finish off.

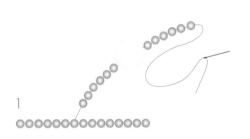
1

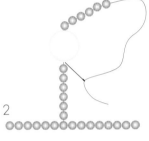
2

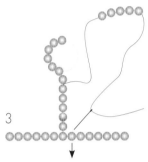
3

4

ADDING THE LOOP:

12 Once again, bring the working thread out of the **seventh** bead along, thread on **25 tone 1 ◎** beads; pass the needle back down through the **eighth** bead along. Pass the needle back through the

loop until you reach the **thirteenth** bead, bring the needle out at that point, pick up **25 more tone 1 ◎** beads, then pass back through the **thirteenth** bead of the initial loop. Continue travelling around both

loops until they feel secure, and do check that your beaded bead fits through both loops, if it doesn't you will need to add a few more seed beads.

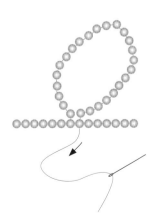

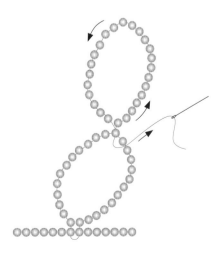

link-by-link lariat

beads you need

- 20g size 8 seed beads
- 10g size 11 seed beads
- Bead soup to match seed beads
- Selection of charms if required
- 0.5m medium link chain
- 8x shell ovals
- Charms (optional)
- Beading needle and thread

1 The larger links are constructed in *tubular herringbone*, using **1m** beading thread.

ROW 1: Pick up **2x size 8 seed beads**, pass the needle back through the first bead so that the two beads 'click' together, thread down through the second bead.

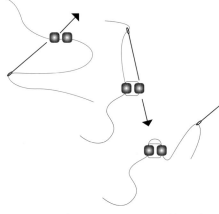

A clever combination of bead weaving, chain and shell ovals that creates a modern look. Skill level: intermediate

2 Pick up a **size 11 seed bead** and pass the needle back through the second bead and **up** through the bead just added. Pick up a **size 11 seed bead**, pass the needle back **down** through the **third** and up through the **fourth** bead.

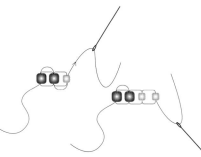

3 Pass the needle back up through the **first bead** and down through the **fourth bead** which brings the **4 beads together** in a square. Finally, pass the needle back **up** through the first bead.

4 **STARTING THE TUBE:**
Pick up **2x size 8 seed beads**, pass the needle **down** through the **second size 8 seed beads** along and **up** through the **first size 11** of the initial ladder. Pick up **2x size 11 seed** beads; pass the needle **down** through the **second size 11 seed bead** of the initial row.

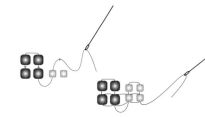

5 **TO STEP UP:**
Pass the needle up through the **first size 8** of **both rows 1 and 2**. This move needs to be repeated after **every four** beads of each row have been added.

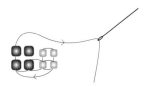

6 Each link has **30 rows** of beads, the initial link can be stitched together (remembering to link through **2x shell ovals** before you do) both through the **11s** and **the size 8 seed beads** to give a complete and seamless circle.

7 There are two sections on each side of the necklace that have **2x shell ovals** linked together with a herringbone tube chain link.

The sections of chain are linked together with a link of **size 11 seed beads** in square stitch working approximately **12 rows** in total before stitching together.

8 THE PENDANT:
A chain link is created as before using both **size 8 seed beads** and **11 seed beads**, this is stitched together. **2x** *square stitch* links are created, before these are stitched together, **2x chain links** are added, these are then stitched on to the main section of the lariat linked with a shell oval and a chain link of **size 11 seed beads** in *square stitch* as before.

9 PENDANT EMBELLISHMENT:
It's playtime! Using the **size 8 seed beads** on the outside of the bottom link, create fringing in a random way with the odd charm if you wish.

daisy, daisy

beads you need
- 4x feature/accent beads
- Up to 225x 4mm pearls (green)
- 16-25x 6mm pearls (daisy centre, pale blue)
- 96-125x 6mm pearls (daisy petals, mid-blue)
- 24x small flower accent beads
- Beading needle and thread

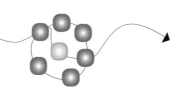

A classic technique with a modern twist with using fashion beads and pearls combined.
Skill level: beginner

necklace

1
Thread up **1.5m beading thread**. *String on **4x 6mm pearls** (petal colour, mid-blue) and **1x 6mm pearl** (centre colour, pale blue). Pass the needle back through the first petal colour pearl in the opposite direction.

2
Pick up the last **2x petal pearls** and take the needle through the **fourth pearl** in the opposite direction. Adjust the beads so that the mid-blue pearls form a circle around the central pale blue pearl, forming your first flower.
NB: To secure the daisy even further, pass the needle back around the beads once again.

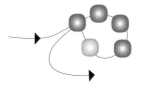

3
Thread on **10x 4mm pearls** (green). Repeat from * to complete a second daisy. Continue repeating daisies and **10x 4mm pearls** until you have four daisies in a row. After the **fourth daisy** has been added, thread on **1x 4mm pearl, 1x large feature bead** and **1x 4mm pearl**. There are four daisies between each of the four large feature beads.

4
To complete the necklace, make a second trip around, passing out through the **first 4mm pearl** after the daisy. Pick up **2x 4mm pearls, 1x flower accent, 2x 4mm pearls, 1x flower accent** and **2x 4mm pearls**. Pass the needle back through the **last 4mm pearl** before the next daisy, then thread around the next daisy ready to place your next 'bridge'. Continue in the same way until the necklace is complete.

bracelet

This is a very relaxing bracelet to make that can be picked up and continued anytime, a good travel project.
Skill level: Beginner

beads you need

- 15g size 11 seed beads in two toning colours
- 4-bar clasp
- KO/Nymo beading thread
- Beading needle

1 Pick up **1x seed bead** (colour 1) pass it down to within 15cm of the tail end of the thread. Pass the needle back through the bead from the tail end upwards **creating a 'stop' bead.** Pick up **2 more size 11s,** same colour and then pick up **3x size 11s** (second colour). Repeat until you have eight sets of three beads in alternating colours.

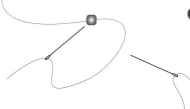

2 **ROW 2:** Pick up **3x size 11 seed beads** (same colour as last three beads on row one). Missing out the last three beads of row one, pass the needle through the **next three seed beads,** continue adding three beads in the same way until you reach the end of the row.

3 Pick up **3x seed beads** to match, the colour at the end of row two. Pass the needle through the **last three beads of row two**. Continue in the same way until row three is complete.

4 Continue adding rows of *three drop peyote*, remembering the pattern is in blocks of three, then change to the opposite colour.

5 **TOP EMBELLISHMENT**
Pick the colour you would like to feature as raised. Pass the needle through the **first three beads of a 'set' of three**. Pick up **3x beads** and pass the needle back through the lower three once again. This helps the beads sit squarely. Pass the needle through the **3 beads next to the first three on the base.** Pick up **3x beads** and pass the needle **through the three base beads** once again. Repeat as before for the third and final set of the block.

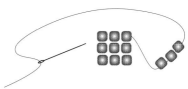

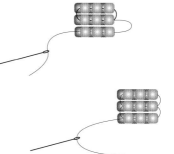

6 Once the first block is finished, you need to join them all together as one. This is done by passing the thread **through the top beads** that have just been put on, then **back through** on **both sides** of all three 'sets' of **top beads.** By doing this they should sit very squarely and tightly together. When the top embellishment is finished just add a bar clasp as opposite.

beads you need

- 15g size 11 purple cylinder beads
- 15g size 11 dark pink cylinder beads
- 10g size 11 light pink cylinder beads
- 4-bar clasp
- KO/Nymo beading thread
- Long beading needle

Square stitch is a great alternative to loom work giving the same effect but without all the ends to tie in.
Skill level: beginner

1 The finished length of the bracelet will be **17.5cm long**, plus the clasp, making **18cm in total.**

First, thread the beading needle with **1.5m** of thread and work *square stitch* (See Figs.1 and 2) over the **21 beads**. See Fig.3 for cuff pattern.

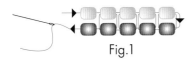

Fig.1

Fig.2

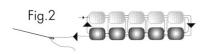

2 When the last row of the pattern has been worked, **repeat** from the **first row** until the cuff is the required length (**0.5cm less than finished length**). It should fit snugly around the wrist.

3 TO COMPLETE:
Match the first fixing point of the clasp to the first **dark pink row** of the cuff. Take the thread through the cuff then through the fixing point several times to add strength. Alternate the stitches through the fixing points and the final row of beads to ensure that it will remain even. Work the thread back through a few rows of beads to secure. Repeat for the other half of the clasp at the other end of the bracelet, matching each end fixing point to a **dark pink row** of beads.

CUFF PATTERN:

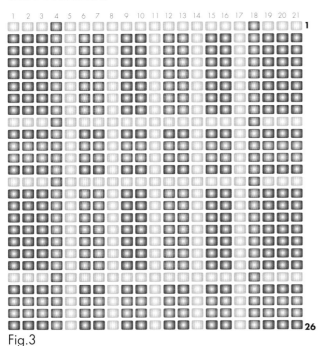

Fig.3

DESIGNER TIP

If the needle is getting tight when returning through each previous row, you can work three rows of pattern then return the needle through the second beaded row. It will give strength and also make beading easier.

regal wraps bracelet

beads you need

- 10g size 8 beads in three colours
- 18-20, 6x4mm cushion crystals
- Bar clasp with 4 fixing points
- Beading needle and thread

Even though this bracelet is worked using size 8 seed beads, it still achieves a delicate effect with the added crystals giving a hint of sparkle.
Skill level: beginner

1 The bracelet is started from a ladder stitch using all three colours of **size 8 beads**. The **first** and the **fifth** pair are in one colour, the **second** and the **fourth** pair are in another and the **third** pair of herringbone rows are in the **third** colour.

3 Pass the needle **down** through the **second** bead added, pick up a **third** bead (in the **second** colour), pass the needle back down through the **second** bead once again and then up through the **third** bead just added. Continue adding beads in the same way until you have added **10** initial beads to the ladder. If the ladder feels a little on the loose side, you can always thread back through the beads which will tighten it up.

2 **ROW 1:**
Thread the needle with **1m** beading thread and thread on **2x size 8 seed beads** (in the **first** colour) to **within 20 cm** from the tail end. Pass the needle back through the **first bead** added and pull up on the thread so that the beads sit side by side.

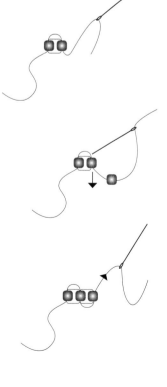

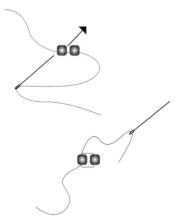

4 STARTING TO HERRINGBONE: ROW 2:

Hold the ladder base with the working thread on the top side of the ladder and the end of the thread hanging downwards. Pick up **2x size 8 beads** (matching the colour of the ladder beads) and pass the needle down through the **next bead** along. Give the two beads a light tap so that they sit fairly flat on top of the base **size 8 beads**. Pass the needle up through the **third size 8 bead** along the ladder, pick up **two** further **size 8s** and pass the needle down through the **next size 8** along (remembering to change colour to match ladder). Continue working in the same way until you reach the end of the ladder.

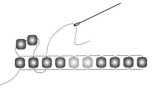

5 TO STEP UP:

Turn your beadwork around so that the **end thread** is hanging back at the **beginning** and pass the needle **back up** through the **ladder bead** next to the **end bead**, then pass the needle up through the **first** bead of the **second row**.

6 ROW 3:

Pick up **two** beads, pass the needle **down** through the next bead along. Then pass the needle **up** through the **first** bead of the second 'pair' along. Continue in the same way for the rest of the row.

7

The fixed edge of the bracelet contains **nine** rows in total; you will need to make **two** of these.

When the two edges are complete it is time to add the long 'columns' of herringbone that make up the centre of the bracelet design. The pairs of **crystals** simply replace a pair of **size 8 seed beads** every so often.

8 HERRINGBONE LENGTHS:

Starting with the centre of the bracelet, start to work *herringbone stitch* but by stacking pairs and just going down by **two** beads each time, then back up **three** beads to add further pairs. The following instructions are where I placed my crystals on the bracelet opposite; this of course can be changed if you wish:

CENTRE ROW: 28 pairs size 8 seed beads; 1x pair crystals; 28 pairs size 8 seed beads.

RIGHT OF CENTRE: 16 pairs size 8 seed beads; 1x pair crystals; 33 pairs size 8 seed beads; 1x pair crystals; 13 pairs size 8 seed beads.

LEFT OF CENTRE: 10 pairs size 8 seed beads; 1x pair crystals; 15 pairs size 8 seed beads; 1x pair of crystals; 24 pairs size 8 seed beads.

OUTSIDE RIGHT: 17 pairs of size 8 seed beads; 1x pair of crystals; 21 pairs of size 8 seed beads; 1x pair of crystals; 23 pairs of size 8 seed beads.

OUTSIDE LEFT: 22 pairs of size 8 seed beads; 1x pair of crystals; 21 pairs of size 8 seed beads; 1x pair of crystals; 17 pairs of size 8 seed beads.

9

As you complete each row of 'pairs' join them onto the other side of the already prepared bracelet end. Pass the needle back and forth three or four times to make sure the joins are secure.

10 ADDING THE CLASP:

Pass the needle up through the **second** bead along on the base row of the ladder at one end of the bracelet. Pass through the end fixing point of the clasp, and **down** through the next **size 8** along, bring the back around these beads again two or three times until things seem secure. Repeat until all four fixing points are secure and then repeat on the other side in the same way.

DESIGNER TIP

It may help to add the clasp when the two ends of the bracelet have been completed so that getting the length of the bracelet correct around the wrist is made easier

chained to love necklace

This design can be altered in many different ways to suit you. It can be a bracelet and if you use smaller beads the chain has a daintier look. A pendant or shape can be suspended from the last link. The choices are endless!
Skill level: intermediate

beads you need

- 30g size 8 seed beads (necklace length)
- 20g size 11 seed beads
- 35x 6mm bi-cone crystals
- 10x 4mm bi-cone crystals
- Beading needle and thread

4
STARTING THE TUBE:
Pass the needle up through the **first size 8** bead once again, pick up **2 x size 8**, pass the needle down through the **second size 8** along and up through the **first size 11** of the initial ladder. Pick up **2 x size 11** beads; pass the needle down through the **second size 11** of the initial row.

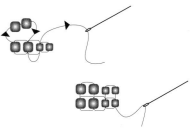

5
TO STEP UP:
Pass the needle up through the **first size 8** of **both rows 1** and **2**. This move needs to be repeated after every **four beads** of **each row** have been added.

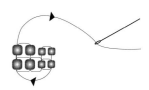

6
Each link has **30 rows** of beads, the initial link can be stitched together both through the **11s** and the **size 8** beads to give a complete and seamless circle. After the initial row they of course have to be linked together then stitched.

Continue making links until you have your required length.

1
The links are constructed in *tubular herringbone*. Using **1m** beading thread, pick up **2 x size 8 seed beads**, pass the needle back through the **first** bead so that the two beads 'click' together, thread down through the **second** bead.

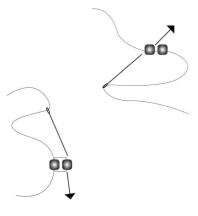

2
Pick up a **size 11 seed bead**, pass the needle back through the **second** bead and up through the bead just added, pick up a **size 11 seed bead**, pass the needle back down through the **third** and up through the **fourth** bead.

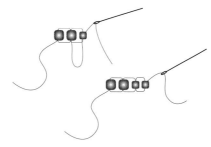

3
Pass the needle back up through the **first** bead and **down** through the **fourth** bead which brings the **4 beads** together in a square. Finally, pass the needle back up through the **first** bead.

7 THE T-BAR CLASP SECTION:

This is constructed in *peyote stitch* using **size 8** seed beads.
Using **1m** beading thread, pick up **1x size 8 bead**, pass the bead down to within **15cm** of the tail end, pass the needle back through the bead creating a **'stop' bead**, thread on **13** more **size 8 beads**.

8

Holding the initial row in your hand, pick up **1x size 8**, pass the needle back through the **second** bead in from the end so that the **first bead** of the **second** row sits below the **last** bead of the **first** row. Continue adding beads in the same manner until you reach the end of the **second** row (remembering to remove the loop from around the 'stop' bead).

Continue adding rows in the same way until you have **7** in total, roll the tube together and run the thread up and down to 'zip' it together.

9

Finally, bring the needle out of one end of the tube, pick up a **4m crystal** and **1x size 11** seed bead, missing out the seed bead, pass the needle back down through the crystal and into the main body of the tube, repeat several times until the crystal feels secure, repeat as before on the other end of the tube.

10 TO FIX THE T-BAR TO THE LINK:

Pass the needle out through a bead in the **centre** of the T-bar beaded piece. Pick up **4x size 8 seed beads**, pass the needle through a bead in a completed link, pass the needle back through the **4x size 8 seed beads**. Continue to pass the needle back and forwards through the beads until the T-bar feels secure remembering to alternate the side of the beads you come in and out of so that the connection sits straight and not at an angle.

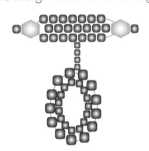

11 CRYSTAL HEART:

The heart is constructed using the *right angle weave* technique, using **6mm crystals** and following the diagrams below. Work one side of the heart, then the other. The sides are linked together with **4mm crystals**.

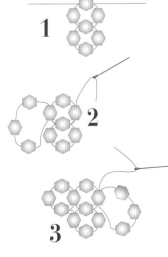

1

2

3

4

5

6

7

8

9

10

11

12 TO ADD THE HEART:

Using a new piece of thread, pick up enough **size 8 beads** to fit around the link and through the top corner of the heart. Pass the needle back through all the beads added and tie together using a double knot. Pass the thread back around several times until the heart feels secure.

fuchsia necklace

necklace

These flowers have natural stunning colours that are bought to life with Japanese delica beads. Either one or two flowers can be worked, the choice is yours.
Skill level: intermediate/advanced

4 Threading the **first** bead of the **second** row on to your thread, position the bead so it sits directly underneath the last right hand bead of the **first** row.

1 Firstly, empty out a small amount of each of the **size 11 delica beads** you will work with. Thread a beading needle with **1.5m** thread.

2 **STARTING SQUARE STITCH:**
Place the fuchsia pattern next to you and note the starting arrow on the grid. Then working from left to right, thread the **first colour bead** down to about **15cm** from the tail end of the thread. Pass the needle back up through the bead creating a 'stop' bead. It may be useful to photocopy chart overleaf at this point.

3 Start with the centre block of the design towards the bottom of the flower; this is because the rows are all the same width with just decreasing down to the tip of the fuchsia.

Thread the first row of beads, there should be **13** beads in total including the 'stop' bead.

5 Pass the needle back through the **last** bead of the **first** row, then turn the needle passing **back through** the **first** bead of the **second** row just added.

Continue along the row adding beads in exactly the same way, being careful to note the colour changes as you work.

6 When the **second** row is complete, pass the needle **back through** the initial row of beads added, then **thread through the second row** once again. This helps to firm up your stitching. The first five rows are exactly the same width as the starting row.

7 SQUARE STITCH DECREASING:
When the previous row is finished prior to the decreasing row, run the threads through as usual, firstly through the row above, then through the row you have just completed. However, instead of running the thread through the entire row, bring the needle out of the bead where you wish to start the next decreased row.

Thread on a bead and **go back** through the bead the thread is coming out of, then **go back through the bead** just added.

8 Continue working towards the base of the fuchsia as before. When this is complete, weave the thread up to the starting row and start to work the pattern upwards. Also create the two green leaves. These are worked with both decreasing and increasing rows.

9 SQUARE STITCH INCREASING:
To increase on either of the outside edges, bring the needle through the **last bead** on the row you wish to increase. Thread on **one** or more beads, **plus the first bead** of the **next** row. Thread **back through** the **increase** bead.

Thread through the **first bead** of the **next** row and continue along in the usual way. You can add as many beads as you wish for an increase, just square stitch your way back into the main section of the beadwork to secure.

10 CONSTRUCTION OF PENDANT AND NECKLACE:
To make the flower look more three-dimensional, I have worked a section of one of the petals again in *square stitch*, and just *stab stitched* it into position over the corresponding petal on the base, this of course is optional. One or two fuchsias stacked, the choice is yours! If you are choosing to have two flowers you need to make a second flower in exactly the same way as the first. You will notice on the pattern that one of the flowers has a tab on it. This actually forms a closed loop behind the flower to hang it from the herringbone rope. It is worked in *square stitch* in the same way as the flower.

11 NECKLACE CONSTRUCTION:
The pendant has been placed on a simple *tubular herringbone rope* using 6 Delica (DB310) beads in total at the ladder base. Using **1m** beading thread, pick up **2x** size 11 seed beads. Pass the needle back through the **first bead** so that the two beads 'click' together. Thread down through the **second** bead.

12 Pick up **1x** size 11 seed bead, pass the needle back through the **second bead** and **up through the bead** just added, **pick up 1x** size 11 seed bead, pass the needle **back down through the third** and **up through the fourth** bead. Continue to add **size 11 seed beads** until you have **six** in total.

13 Pass the needle **back up** though the **first** bead and **down through** the **sixth** bead which brings all **six beads together** into a circle. Finally, pass the needle **back up** through the **first** bead.

fuchsia necklace

14 **STARTING THE TUBE:**
Pass the needle up through the
first size 11 seed bead once
again, pick up **2x size 11 seed
beads**, pass the needle **down**
through the **second size 11** along
and **up** through the **third size 11**
and pick up **2x size 11** and pass
down through the **fourth size 11** of
the initial row, add **1x** further pair
of **size 11 seed beads** to complete
the second row.

15 **TO STEP UP:**
Pass the needle **up** through the
first **size 11** of **both rows 1
and 2**. This move needs to be
repeated after every **6** beads of
each row have been added.

Continue adding 'pairs' of
beads until the required length is
produced. Thread the pendant on
to the necklace length and attach
the clasp you have chosen to the
necklace ends.

16 **CUFF BRACELET:**
Work the cuff bracelet in *square
stitch* as before, adding the same
amounts of increase on each side
as you go. Attach a clasp to finish
in the usual way.

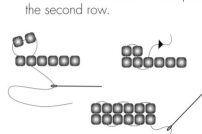

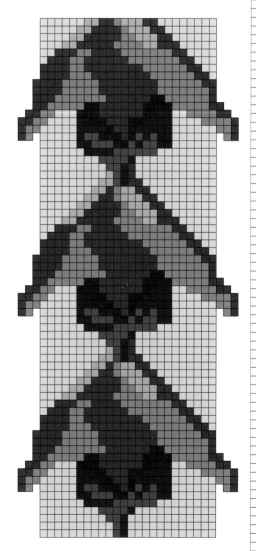

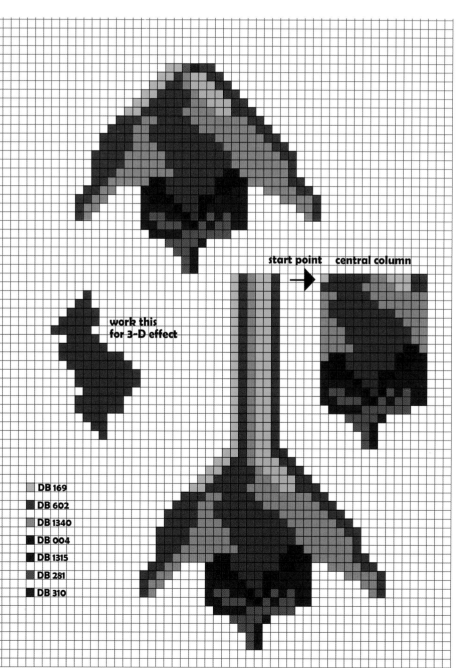

work this
for 3-D effect

start point   central column

DB 169
DB 602
DB 1340
DB 004
DB 1315
DB 281
DB 310

flower power chain necklace

beads you need

- 30g size 5 triangles
- 30g size 8 triangles (or seed beads)
- 150 4mm pearls
- 20g size 11 seed beads
- 2 x flower accent beads with a hole through the centre
- Beading needle and thread

NB: These amounts are dependent on the length of necklace that you make

This is a great necklace for using those larger feature beads that you love but have no idea which project to use them in.
Skill level: beginner

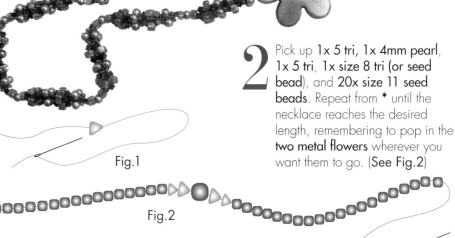

1 As you thread the base of the necklace, the two metal accent beads can be added in at any point. Thread a beading needle with **1.5m beading thread**. Pass *1x size 8 triangle down to within **15cm** of the tail end of the thread; pass the needle back through the bead creating a 'stop' bead. (See Fig.1)

Fig.1

2 Pick up **1x 5 tri**, **1x 4mm pearl**, **1x 5 tri**, **1x size 8 tri** (or seed bead), and **20x size 11 seed beads**. Repeat from * until the necklace reaches the desired length, remembering to pop in the **two metal flowers** wherever you want them to go. (See Fig.2)

Fig.2

3 The model shown has 7 bead sections, flower 14 bead sections and flower which gives an asymmetric look. When the base is complete, you need to double knot both ends together forming a continuous necklace.

4 **TOP EMBELLISHMENT**
Pass the needle through the **first set of triangles and pearls**, and through the **first five of the 20 seed beads**. Thread on **1x size 11, 1x 4mm pearl** and **1x size 11 seed bead**. Pass the needle back through the **first five seed beads** once again, forming a loop of beads around the seed beads. **Repeat this three more times** until you have **four loops** sitting around the **first five seed beads**. (See Fig.3)

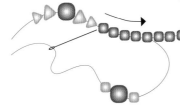

Fig.3

5 Pass the needle through the next **five seed beads** along. Thread on *1x size 8 tri, 1x size 5 tri and 1x size 8 tri (or seed bead). Pass the needle back through the **five seed beads**. Repeat from * until **four sets have been added** in total.

6 Thread through the next **five** and **repeat the first set** once again using **seed, pearl, seed**, and finally through the **last five** using **8 tri, 5 tri and 8 tri**.

Continue this embellishment along the length of the necklace. I slipped a size **8 tri**, pearl and size **8 tri** into the **centre** of the **two flowers** as I beaded.

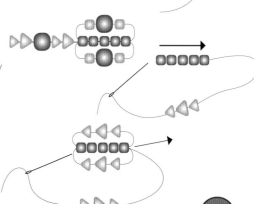

art nouveau necklace

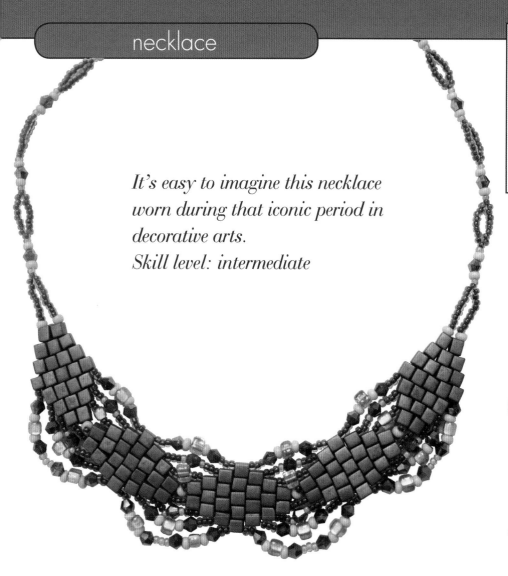

It's easy to imagine this necklace worn during that iconic period in decorative arts.
Skill level: intermediate

beads you need

- 15g 4mm cubes
- 2x 10g size 11 seed beads in two colours
- 1x size 8 seed beads
- 5g size 5 triangles
- 50-60 4mm bi-cones
- Beading needle and thread
- 2-bar clasp

5 Thread the needle back up through the **third cube** so that it is in the correct position to add the next cube.

6 Add **two more cubes** in the same way so that there are a total of five cubes on this first row.

7 **ADDING MORE ROWS: TO START ROW 2:** the thread should be coming out of the top of the last cube added. Pick up **two cubes**, and take the needle through the **second loop** of the thread along the initial ladder from **back to front**.

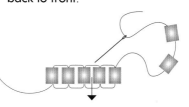

8 Allowing the two new cubes to sit side by side with the holes facing upwards, take the needle back up through the first new cube.

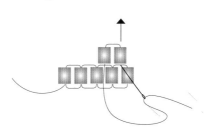

1 First, **five *brick stitch*** diamond shapes need to be constructed. Thread a beading needle with **1m** beading thread. Empty a small amount of cubes on to your beading mat. Thread **two cubes** down to within **15cm of the tail** end of the thread, and bring the needle back through the first cube.

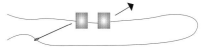

2 Pull the ends of the thread in the opposite directions so that the cubes 'click' together snugly side by side.

3 Holding the beads between the thumb and forefinger, take the needle back through the second cube once again.

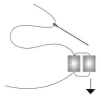

4 Pick up a cube; take the needle **back through** the **second** cube added. Pull the thread through and down towards the tail end until the **third bead** sits next to the **second cube**.

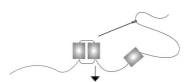

9 Take the needle back down through the second new cube, then under the loop that sits on top of the cube once more.

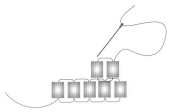

10 Take the needle back up through the **second cube** once again. These moves at the beginning of each row form a **'locking'** stitch that will help to anchor the first cube and stop it tipping inwards so that you can achieve a flat, even piece of beadwork. Row 2 contains 4 cubes.

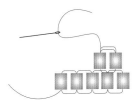

11 **STARTING ROW 3:** add **two cubes** in the same way as before, threading the needle under the **second loop** in from the end of **row 2.** Complete the row adding **one cube** at a time. Row 3 contains three cubes.

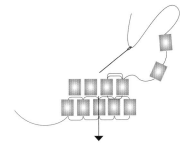

12 **ROW 4:** contains **two cubes** and is worked by just making the **'locking'** stitch.

13 When row 4 is complete, you need to thread back through to one of the outer cubes of the initial row and work a mirror image of the design in exactly the same way. Four further diamond cubes need to be worked as the base of the necklace.

14 **STRINGING THE NECKLACE TOGETHER: ROW 1:** Place the initial 'diamond' shape in a horizontal position and pass the needle through the top cube of the two sitting at the end of the diamond. Thread on **1x size 11, 1x size 8** and **1x size 11 seed bead.** Pass the needle through the corresponding cube of the second diamond shape and continue along adding this first set of beads between each diamond shape.

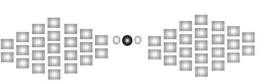

15 **ROW 2:** Pass the needle through the second cube up on the diamond and thread on **2x size 11, 1x size 5 triangle** and **2x size 11 seed beads.** Pass the needle through the corresponding cube on the next diamond shape along. Repeat across all the diamond shapes.

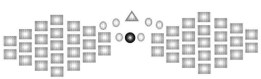

16 **ROW 3:** Pass the needle through the third cube up on the diamond and thread on **3x size 11, 1x size 11, 1x 4mm crystal, 1x size 11** and **3x size 11 seed beads.** Pass the needle through the corresponding cube on the next diamond shape along. Repeat as before.

17 **ROW 4:** Pass the needle through the top cube on the first diamond. Thread on **3x size 11, 1x 4mm crystal, 1x size 8, 1x size 5 triangle, 1x size 8, 1x 4mm crystal** and **3x size 11 seed beads.** Pass the needle through the corresponding cube on the next diamond shape along. Repeat as before.

This now concludes the top part of the stringing for the necklace.

DESIGNER TIP

It is very tempting to string all of the diamonds together at this point (row 4 of stringing the necklace together) across the top but DON'T! If you do, you will alter the tension and your necklace will not sit flat around the neck.

necklace

18 **STRINGING THE BOTTOM 'SWAGS':**
This is done in exactly the same way as the top section only the make-up of the beads is slightly different. Once again there are four rows starting from the lower of the two cubes at the end of the initial diamond, working downwards to complete. NB The bottom swags are completely different from the top swags.

ROW 1: 4x size 11 seed beads.

ROW 3: 3x size 11, 1x 4mm crystal, 1 x size 8, 1x size 5 tri, 1x size 8, 1x 4mm crystal and 3 size 11 seed beads.

ROW 2: 3x size 11, 1x size 11, 1x 4mm crystal, 1x size 11 and 3x size 11 seed beads.

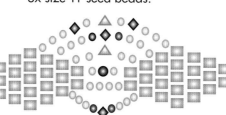

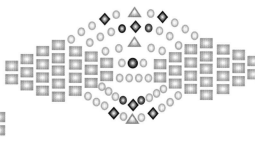

ROW 4: 2x size 11, 1x 4mm crystal, 1x size 8, 1x size 5 tri, 1x size 8, 1x 4mm crystal, 3x size 11, 1x 4mm crystal, 1x size 8, 1x size 5 tri, 1x size 8, 1x 4mm crystal and 2x size 11 seed beads. This now completes the 'swags' for the bottom section of the necklace.

19 **TO FINISH:**
The final portion of the necklace is kept fairly simple as the centre section is the 'star' of the show!
This is constructed by passing the needle through one of the two end cubes on the last diamond shape, thread on 1x size 8 *10x size 11, 1x size 11, 1x size 8, 1x 4mm crystal, 1x size 8, 1x size 11.

20 Repeat from * until the necklace reaches the correct length. The last section consists of **10 size 11, 1x size 11** and **1x size 8.** Pass the needle through the fixing point that corresponds with the cube used then run the thread back down through all the beads just added, when you reach the cubes once again, pass the needle back down through the cube and up through the cube sitting to the side of it.

21 Thread on **1x size 8** and **9x size 11 seed beads.** Pass the needle through the last of the **10 initial seed beads** on the **initial** row, 1x size 11, 1x size 8, 1x 4mm crystal, 1x size 8, 1x size 11 and 1x size 11. From now on you will be adding **8x size 11 seed beads** in between each intersection of seeds and crystals. Repeat in exactly the same way for the other side of the necklace.

vintage blue butterfly necklace

beads you need

- 4x 5g size 11 delica seed beads
- 18x24 3mm bi-cone crystals
- 1x small toggle clasp
- Beading needle and thread

1 Work the butterfly shape in both increasing and decreasing *square stitch*. Refer to **Autumn Leaves design** (p42) for increasing and decreasing instructions

2 **ADDING THE CRYSTALS TO THE LOWER WING TIPS AND BODY:**
Pass the needle **down** through the **right hand** side bead at the base of the body, *square stitch* 12 more dark purple beads in a single line. Pick up *1x pink, 1x crystal, 1x pink and 1x purple. Missing out the last purple, thread back up through the **pink, crystal** and **pink** and thread up through the **12 purple beads** and over the bead on the bottom left side of the body. Repeat in the same way, this time adding **8 purple beads** before repeating the crystal section from * to complete.

No summer outfit would be complete without this charming little necklace. Skill level: beginner

3 **THE LOWER WINGS:**
Simply pass the needle through the **last bead** of the **lower wing** and thread on **1x pink, 1x crystal** and **1x pink**, missing out the last pink. Thread back up through the crystal and pink before entering the body of the wing once again. Repeat on the other side.

DESIGNER TIP

When each row is completed, remember to thread the needle back through the beads just added to secure as you would with *flat square stitch*!

4 **THE NECKLACE STRAPS:**
Pass the needle out of the very **top bead** on one side of the **upper wing**, using the purple beads. Pick up **20 purple seeds**, *1x white, 1x crystal and 1x white. Pick up a further **20 purple beads**, repeat from * until the necklace is the correct length. String on the final **20 seed beads** and pass the needle through the fixing point of the clasp and down through the last white added. Thread on **20 pink seed beads**, pass the needle through **white, crystal, white** and continue until you arrive back at the wing end. (See Fig.1)

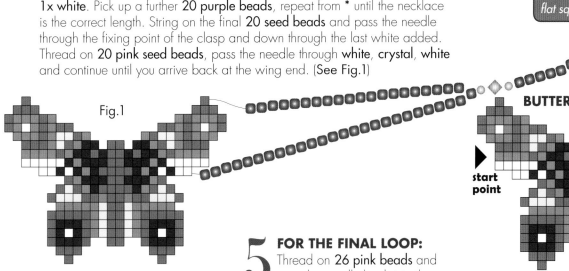

Fig.1

BUTTERFLY PATTERN:

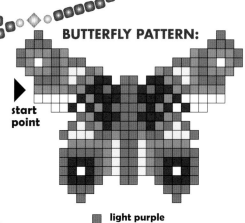

start point

5 **FOR THE FINAL LOOP:**
Thread on **26 pink beads** and pass the needle back into the butterfly at the point shown. Repeat for the other side of the necklace in exactly the same way.

- ▬ light purple
- ▬ dark purple - DB 310
- ▬ pink - DB 047
- ☐ white - DB 167

captured beauty necklace

necklace

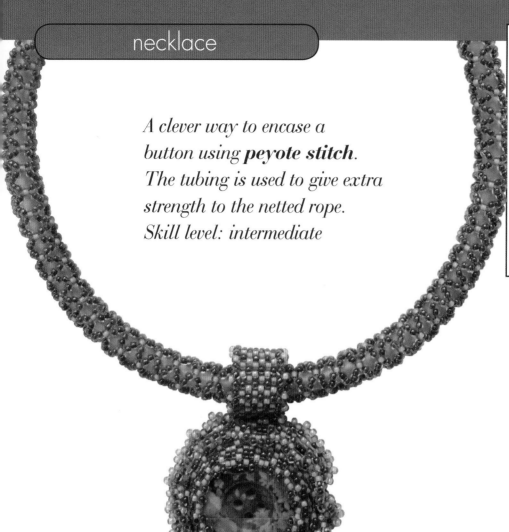

*A clever way to encase a button using **peyote stitch**. The tubing is used to give extra strength to the netted rope.*
Skill level: intermediate

beads you need

Rope:
- Necklace length of plastic tube 5mm wide
- Plastic tubing fastener
- 20g size 11 seed beads (main colour)
- 10g size 11 seed beads (accent colour)

Pendant:
- 1x 2.5cm button
- 10g x3 toning colours of size 11 seed beads
- Beading needle and thread

3 Pick up **2x main**, **1x accent** and **2x main** seed beads, pass the needle down through the **first accent bead** on the **first** loop completed on the **second** row.

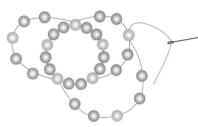

Continue adding loops as you work the netted tube. There is no need to 'step down' as you will be spiralling naturally.

1 **ROPE CONSTRUCTION:**
the stitch used is *tubular netting* which is worked around the plastic tubing.
Pick up **1x accent colour** and **2x main colour** until you have **15 beads** in total. Make a circle with the beads and then wrap the beads around the plastic tubing and tie in a double knot. Take the needle through the first accent bead once again.

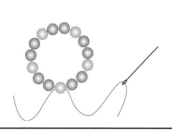

2 Pick up **2x main**, **1x accent** and **2x main** seed beads, pass the needle through the **second accent bead** along, add a **second loop** in the same way.

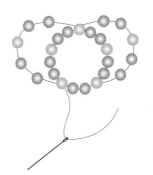

4 **PENDANT CONSTRUCTION:**
the pendant is worked in flat, circular *peyote stitch*, around the button; I found it helpful to alternate the three chosen colours as you progress through the design.

ROW 1:

Thread on **40 seed beads**, pass the needle back through the beads from the tail end upwards, and pass the needle back through the first bead added.

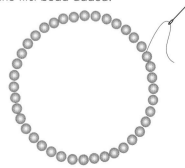

5 Thread on **one bead** (in the second row colour) it will sit over the **second** bead of **row 1**, pass the needle through the third bead of row 1.
Continue with *peyote stitch* in the same way until you reach the **end of row 2**, step up.

6
ROW 3: Work *peyote stitch* in your third chosen colour adding one bead, step up.
ROW 4: Work *peyote stitch* in your first colour once again, step up.
ROW 5: This time, add **2 beads** between each bead of the **fourth** row, step up.
ROW 6: Add **1 bead** between each pair of beads from **row 5**, step up.
ROW 7: Add **2 beads** between each bead added in **row 6**, step up.
Place the button in the centre and on top of your beading.
NB Whilst working the next 3 rows, you need to be pulling up on your tension and encouraging your beadwork to encase the button.
ROW 8: Add **1 bead** between each pair added in **row 7**, step up.
ROW 9: Add **1**, then **2 beads** alternately between each bead added in **row 8**, step up.
ROW 10: Add **1 bead** between each **single and pair** of beads added in **row 9**, step up. After the step up, work a double knot between the beads to anchor the work firmly. Pass the needle down through to the **second** row from the base row that has 2 beads added at one time (row 6).
ROW 11: Pass the needle through **one pair** of beads, add **1 bead** between each **pair of beads**, step up.
NB You are now beading outwards, creating the side frills of the pendant.
ROW 12: Add **2 beads** between each bead of **row 11**, step up.
ROW 13: Add **2 beads** between each pair of beads on **row 12**, step up.
ROW 14: Add **1 bead** between each pair added in last row, step up – and between each individual bead.
ROW 15: Add **2 beads** between each bead of **row 15**, the first frill is now complete.

TO MAKE THE SECOND FRILL

Start at the back of the button, pass the needle through the **fourth** row from the start of you original beading which is the **first** row of added 'pairs' of beads. Pass the needle through a **pair of beads**.
ROW 1: Place **1 bead** between each pair, step up.
ROW 2: Place **2 beads** between each bead of row 1, step up.
ROW 3: Add **1 bead**, step up (once again, you are now working outwards).
ROW 4: Add **2 beads**, step up.
ROW 5: Add **2 beads**, step up.
ROW 6: Add **2 beads**, step up.
ROW 7: Add **2 beads**, step up.
ROW 8: Add **2 beads**, step up.
ROW 9: Add **2 beads**, and **1 bead** alternately between each pair, step up.

ROW 10: Add **1 bead** between each bead (including each pair) to finish the second frill.

7
TO MAKE THE BAIL:
This is worked off the edge of the second frill in *one drop peyote* 6 beads across. It needs to be long enough for the netted tubing to fit through, when the correct length is reached, simply fold over and peyote into place on the back of the frill. A small picot edge was also added to the sides of the bail to echo the frills around the button.

herringbone bracelet

beads you need

- Size 8 seed beads
- A few size 11 beads in toning colours
- Magatama mix
- Magnetic clasp
- Nymo thread
- Beading needle

*This chunky bracelet is a great introduction to **tubular herringbone**. Skill level: beginner*

3 Join the bead ladder into a circle making sure the holes on one side of the beads are facing upwards and the work is not twisted in any way.

4 **STARTING THE HERRINGBONE:**
ROW 2: Holding the **base** circle of beads with the working thread on the top of the circle and the end of the thread hanging downwards, pick up **2 size 8 seed beads** and pass the needle **down** through the **next bead** along. Give the two beads a slight tap so that they sit fairly flat on top of the base **size 8 beads**, pass the needle **up** through the **third size 8 bead** along the ladder, pick up a further **2 size 8s** and pass the needle **down** through the next **size 8** along. Continue working in the same way until you reach the first pair added.

1 The bracelet is started from a *ladder stitch* using **8 size 8** seed beads.

ROW 1: Thread the needle with **1m** beading thread, Thread on **2 size 8 seed beads** to within **20 cm** from the tail end. Pass the needle back through the first bead added and pull up on the thread so that the beads sit side by side.

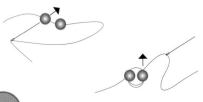

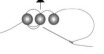
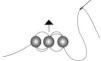

2 Pass the needle **down** through the **second** bead added, pick up a **third** bead, pass the needle back down through the **second** bead once again then up through the **third** bead just added. Continue adding beads in the same way until you have added **all 8 initial beads** to the ladder. If the ladder feels a little on the loose side, you can always thread back through the beads to tighten it up.

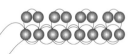

5 **TO STEP UP:**
Now that the first row of herringbone is complete you need to 'step up'. This is done by passing the needle up through both the first bead of the initial ladder and the first bead of the first pair on the row just completed.

vintage blue
butterfly necklace

butterfly pattern

Monet's
poppy necklace

poppy pattern

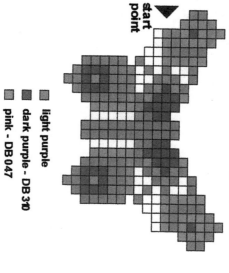

OOPS!

One of our lovely readers found an error on the butterfly chart so here it is again, corrected!

start point

☐ light purple

☐ dark purple - DB 310

☐ pink - DB 047

☐ white - DB 157

OOPS!
An error on the poppy chart.

On the main poppy chart the centre (number 3) should be purple and DB654 is of course red not yellow!

necklace join

necklace join

start point

start point

start point

start point

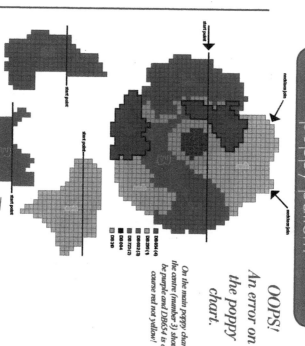

☐ DB654 (4)
☐ DB291 (1)
☐ DB602 (3)
☐ DB721 (2)
☐ DB004
☐ DB310

6 **ROW 3:** Thread on **2 size 8 beads**, pass the needle **down** through the **next size 8** of the pair, then thread the needle **up** through the **first** bead of the next pair along. This creates a **'linking'** stitch between each of the pairs as you work. Continue adding pairs with linking stitches until you reach the first pair once again.

7 **ADDING MAGATAMAS:** The next row is worked in exactly the same way only this time instead of using size 8 seed beads they are replaced with **magatama drops**. Treat them in the same way but make sure that the drop end of the bead is facing outwards as you work. Continue adding Magatamas **every three rows**.

Once the first three or four rows are added the beadwork becomes easier to hold.

8 **JOINING A NEW THREAD:** This is very straightforward. Run a new thread up through the line of beads, double knotting between two beads about four rows down from where you wish to emerge to continue beading. Finish off the old thread in the same way, returning back down towards the start of the bracelet, double knot, then cut off.

9 **TO COMPLETE:** When the bracelet reaches the required length, join the pairs of beads together into a ladder exactly the same way as for the start.

Using **size 11 seed beads**, work *brick stitch* through the loops of the completed ladder. This creates a nice neat end.

10 **BRICK STITCH:** Bring the needle through any one of the **size 8 seed beads** on the ladder. Pick up **1 size 11 seed bead**, pass the needle **through the loop** which holds the ladder together then pass the needle **back up** through the size 11 bead.

11 Continue picking up **1x size 11 seed bead**, passing the needle through the **next loop** along then passing the needle **up** through the bead once again until you reach the first bead added again.

Take one end of the clasp and sew on to the circle of brick stitch. Attach at opposite sides of the circle going through the clasp several times. Attaching at opposite sides makes the clasp sit in the middle of the hole in a central position.

12 When the clasp is firmly attached, work a further **2 rows of brick stitch** creating a nice neat finish. Repeat at other side. You may wish to add a safety chain to your bracelet. To do this, simply thread through any of the **size 11 beads**, then string on further **size 11s** which will need to be long enough to slip the bracelet on to your wrist.

13 Complete by attaching to a **size 11** on the opposite side of the bracelet.

14 **PLEASE NOTE:** Magnetic clasps are unsuitable for people fitted with pacemakers; they also love to attach themselves to supermarket trolleys! You have been warned!

DESIGNER TIP
As the size 8 seed beads are quite a lot larger than the size 11 seed beads you will probably find that you need to work 2 size 11 seed beads into 1 loop between each size 8 which works well.

lattice bracelet

The cubes in this bracelet provide a rigid frame for the lattice centre.
Skill level: beginner

beads you need

- 20g 4mm cubes
- 10g size 11 seed beads
- 10g size 8 seed beads
- 4mm crystals (22-35)
- Beading needle and thread
- Bar clasp with 3 fixing points

1 Make two ladders using the **4mm cube** beads, long enough to fit around your wrist allowing a small gap for the clasp.

Using about **1m** of beading thread, pick up **2x 4mm cubes**, pass them down to within **15cm** of the tail end of the working thread.

2 Pass the needle back through the **first cube** added, then back down through the **second cube**, this will ensure the cubes to sit together side by side.

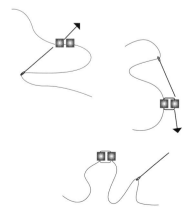

3 Pick up a **third cube**, pass the needle back down through the **second cube** then back up through the cube just added.

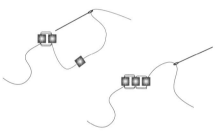

4 Continue to add cubes in this way until your line of cubes is the correct length. Make a second length in exactly the same way. **NB Make sure you have an even number of cubes on each ladder.**

5 **TO JOIN THE LADDERS:** Pass the needle down through the **second cube** from the end of one ladder, thread on **two cubes**, pass the needle down through the end cube.

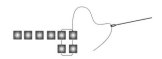

6 Thread the needle down through the **two cubes**, add **two more cubes**, pass the needle back down through the other **two cubes**. Carry on adding 'pairs' of cubes until you have **six pairs** in total. Join the **second ladder** to the ends of the block of cubes just created.

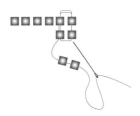

Repeat in exactly the same way for the other end of the bracelet.

7 ADDING THE LATTICE SECTION:
Manipulate the working thread so that it comes out of the **third cube** along at either end (**ladder 1**).

8 Thread on **4x size 11 beads**, **1x size 8 bead**, **1x crystal**, **1x size 8 bead** and **4x size 11 beads**. Pass the needle down through the **fourth cube** along on the **second ladder of cubes** created (**ladder 2**).

9 Bring the needle up through the **third cube** along (**ladder 2**), thread on **3x size 11 beads** and pass the needle through the **size 8 bead, crystal** and **size 8 bead** already added. Thread on **3x size 11 beads**, pass the needle up through the **fourth cube** along (**ladder 1**).

10 Continue adding further 'crosses' of beads until you have two cubes left on both sides of the ladders.

11 TO ADD THE PICOT:
Pass the needle up through the **first cube** on the ladder, thread on **3x size 11 seed beads**. Pass the needle under the **next loop** along, then pass the needle **up through** the **third seed bead**.

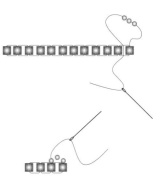

12 Pick up **2x size 11** seed beads, pass the needle under the **next loop** along, then through the **second** of the beads just added.

Continue to add the picot edge on both sides of the ladder.

13 ADDING THE CLASP:
Position the clasp against the side of the bracelet length. Decide which beads sit next to the fixing points of the clasp, bring the thread out next to the fixing point and pass the needle through the fixing point then back into the nearest available bead. Do this two or three times to make sure the clasp is secure. Repeat in the same way for each fixing point.

crystal splendour bracelet

beads you need

- 2 strands 6mm pearls (36-50)
- 1 strand 8mm pearls (18-25)
- 2 strands 4x6mm cushion crystals (56-65)
- 10g size seed beads
- 10g size 8 seed beads
- S-lon beading thread and needle
- 2-bar clasp

Plenty of sparkle makes this bracelet one of the stars of the show. Skill level: beginner

1 The base of the bracelet is made of circles of beads using the *right angle weave* technique. Thread the beading needle with **1.5m** beading thread, pick up **1x crystal, 1x 8mm pearl, 1x crystal, 1x size 11 seed bead, 1x 6mm pearl, 1x size 11 seed bead, 1x crystal, 1x 8mm pearl, 1x crystal, 1x size 11 seed bead, 1x 6mm pearl** and **1x size 11 seed bead.** These beads form the first circle. (See Fig. 1)

2 Pass the needle back through all the beads added to form the circle. Tie the threads in a double knot to secure. Pass the needle through the **crystal, 8mm pearl** and **crystal.** Pick up **1x size 11 seed bead, 1x 6mm pearl, 1x size 11 seed bead, 1 x crystal, 1x 8mm pearl, 1x crystal, 1x size 11 seed bead, 1x 6mm pearl** and **1x size 11 seed bead.** Pass the needle back through the **crystal, 8mm pearl** and **crystal** to form a **second** circle attached to the **first** circle. Continue in this way until the bracelet reaches the correct length for your wrist. (See Fig. 2)

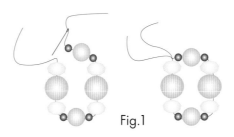

Fig.1

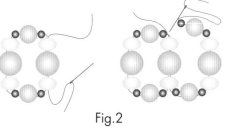

Fig.2

3 Working along one edge of the bracelet, place a **size 8** seed bead in between each of the two size 11 seed beads already in place on the bracelet base. Repeat in the same way for the opposite side of the bracelet. (See Fig. 3)

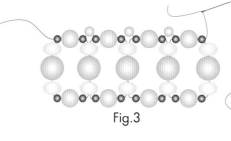

Fig.3

4 **CRISS-CROSS PATTERN**
Pass the needle through the first **size 8 bead** along one side of the bracelet, pick up **5x size 11s, 1x crystal** and **5x size 11s.** Pass the needle through the next diagonal **size 8** on the opposite side of the bracelet. Continue in this way until the row is complete, forming a line of zig-zags. (See Fig. 4)

DESIGNER TIP

To anchor the end half-stitch, you will need to pass the needle through the size 11 seed bead as there is no size 8 sitting at either end of the bracelet base.

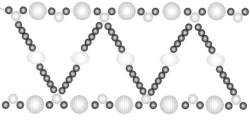

Fig.4

5 When the first line of zig-zags is complete you will need to add the second half which will complete the cross over. This is done by bringing the thread out of the corresponding bead at the end of the bracelet. Pick up **5x size 11 seed beads**, pass the needle through the **crystal** in the middle of the first crossover, pick up another **5x size 11 seed beads** and pass the needle through the next **size 8** along on the other side of the bracelet. This move completes the crosses on the top of the bracelet. (**See Fig. 5**)

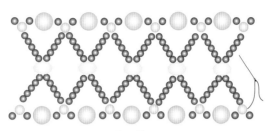

Fig.5

6 **TO FINISH:**
Simply Add a 2-bar clasp by fixing it to both sides of the 8mm pearl at each end of the bracelet.

Twist and shout bracelet

beads you need
- 10g size 11 seed beads for the core
- 20g size 11 seed bead mix for the outside edge beading

A traditional beading technique given a modern twist: Skill level: beginner

1 **CREATING THE SPIRAL ROPE:**
Pick up **4 core colour** beads (**colour A**) and 3 outside edge beads (**colour B**). Tie the beads into a circle. Pass the needle back up through the **4A** (**Fig.1**). Pick up **1A** and **3B*** and let the beads drop down to the work (**Fig.2**). Pass the needle up through the last **3A** and the **A** just added, pull the thread up firmly (**Fig.3**).

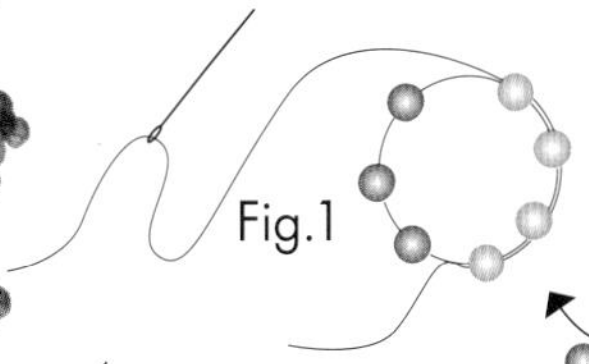

Fig.1

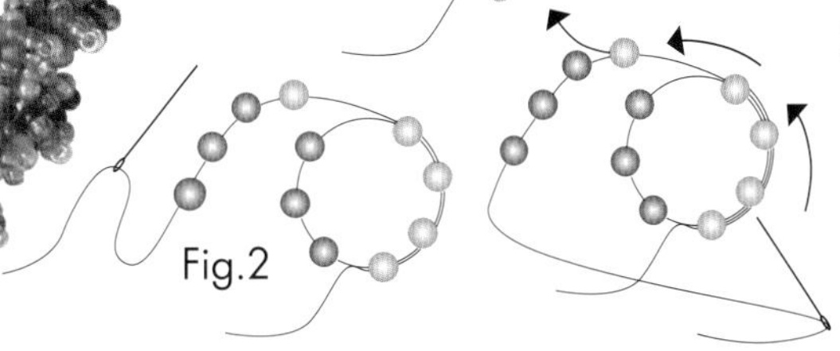

Fig.2

Place the beads just added so that they sit next to the three previous outside beads. Pick up **1A** and **3B** and **repeat from *** until you have reached the required length.

2 **TOP EMBELLISHMENT**
At the tail end of the bracelet length, bring the needle **down** through the **first set of three outside beads** on the spiral (**Fig.3**). Thread on **7x size 11 mix beads**, pass the needle **back up** through the **3 beads** once again (**Fig.4**). Thread on **3x size 11 mix beads**, pass the needle **down** through the **second set of three beads** (**Fig.5**).

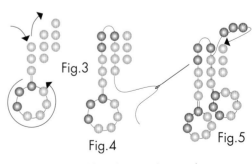

Fig.3

Fig.4

Fig.5

3 Keep adding loops of **7 seed beads** at the **base** of **every set of 3 outside beads**, and add **3x seed beads** forming a bridge as you thread down through the next set of three beads, continue until the whole bracelet is embellished.

autumn leaves necklace

This necklace gives you a great chance to play with colour mixing, as well as creating your own toggle clasp. Skill level: intermediate

beads you need

- Delica size 11 seed beads
  10g DB 124
  10g DB 144
  10g DB 272
  10g DB 501
  10g DB 794
- 5x 4mm bi-cone crystals
- KO beading thread
- Beading needle

2 **STARTING THE HERRINGBONE TUBE:**
Thread the needle with **1m** beading thread. Thread on **2x 794** beads to within **20cm** of the tail end. Pass the needle back through the first bead added and pull up on the thread so that the beads sit side by side.

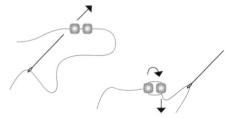

3 Pass the needle **down** through the **second** bead added, pick up a **third** bead, pass the needle **back down** through the **second bead** again and then up through the **third bead** just added.

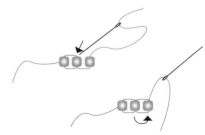

4 Continue adding beads in the same way until you have added **all 6** initial beads to the ladder. If the ladder feels a little on the loose side you can thread back through the beads to tighten it up

1 The necklace base is constructed in *tubular herringbone*. All 5 colours listed are incorporated into the necklace base in the following order: **794 / 144 / 501 / 272 / 124.**

The first 2.5cm of the tube is worked solidly in **794**. When the following rows are added, place **1x 144** at different places on the next few rows gradually building up until the tube changes its entire colour to **144**. Work a solid inch of **144**, then start to slowly add the next colour **501**. Continue in the same way until all the colours are added. If the necklace base is not long enough simply reverse the colours i.e. the last colour added is **124** – start to slowly add **272** once again working backwards along the number line until the necklace is the correct length.

5

Join the bead ladder into a circle making sure the holes on one side of the beads are facing upwards and the work is not twisted in any way.

6

Holding the base circle of beads with the working thread on the top of the circle and the end of the thread hanging downwards, pick up **2x 794** beads and pass the needle **down** through the next bead along. Give the two beads a slight tap so that they sit fairly flat on top of the base size 11 beads. Pass the needle **up** through the **third size 11 bead** along the ladder and pick up a further **2x size 11s** and pass the needle **down** through the next **size 11** along. Add the last pair of beads in the same manner.

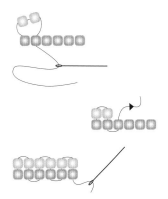

7 TO STEP UP:

Now that the first row of *herringbone* is complete you need to 'step up' . This is done by passing the needle up through **both** the **first** bead of the initial ladder and the **first** bead of the **first pair** on the row just completed.

8 ROW 3:

Thread on **2 size 11** beads and pass the needle **down** through the next **size 11** of the pair. Then thread the needle **up** through the **first bead** of the **next pair** along. This creates a 'linking' stitch between each of the pairs as you work. Continue adding pairs with linking stitches until you reach the first pair once again.

Continue adding rows in the same way remembering to change colour as you work. Also feel free to experiment with blending the colours. It is really simple and as long as you gradually change colour you will avoid blocks of colour.

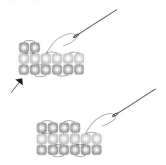

9 JOINING A NEW THREAD:

This is very straightforward. Just run a new thread up through the line of beads, double-knotting between two beads about four rows down from where you wish to emerge to continue beading. Finish off the old thread in the same way, returning back down towards the start of the necklace, double knot, then cut off.

10 FINISHED NECKLACE LENGTH:

When you have reached the correct length to fit, place the herringbone tube to one side as we need to make the leaves before adding the T-bar and loop to finish.

11 CONSTRUCTION OF LEAVES:

All the leaves are worked in *square stitch* using the same colours that are incorporated into the necklace base. The basic shape for each of the leaves is shown on the chart. There are **10 leaves** on the necklace in total, but you can add more or less, the choice is entirely yours.

Below is a list of the colour combinations used for the original necklace:
Work **2x** leaves with **144** inner and **272** outer.
Work **1x** leaf with **144** inner and **794** outer.
Work **2x** leaves with **124** inner and **501** outer.
Work **1x** leaf with **501** inner and **794** outer.
Work **2x** leaves with **144** inner and **501** outer.
Work **1x** leaf with **794** inner and **144** outer.
Work **1x** leaf with **272** inner and **501** outer.

12 SQUARE STITCH LEAVES:

Firstly, empty a small amount of the first two colours to be used on to your beading mat. Thread a beading need with **1m** beading thread.

13 STARTING TO SQUARE STITCH:

Place the leaf pattern next to you and note the starting arrow on the grid, then working from left to right, thread on the first colour bead down to about **10cm** from the tail end of the thread. Pass the needle **back up** through the bead creating a **'stop'** bead.

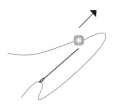

necklace

14 Continue to thread on this entire first row of beads, there should be **12** beads in total including the 'stop' bead.

15 Threading the **first** bead of the **second** row onto your thread, position the bead so that it sits directly underneath the **last right hand bead** of the **first row**.

16 Pass the needle back through the **last** bead of the **first** row and then turn the needle passing **back** through the first bead of the **second row** just added.

17 Continue along the row adding beads in exactly the same way, being careful to note the colour changes as you work.

18 When the second row is complete, pass the needle **back through** the **initial row** of beads added and then thread through the **second row** once again.

Threading through the two rows gives extra stability to the beads and brings them nicely into line. Continue to add rows in the same manner.

19 **SQUARE STITCH – DECREASING ON THE OUTSIDE EDGES:**
When the previous row is finished prior to the decreasing row, run the threads through as usual; firstly through the row above and then through the row you have just completed. However, instead of running the thread through the entire row, bring the needle out of the bead you wish to start the next decrease row.

20 **NECKLACE CONSTRUCTION:**
When all **10** leaves are completed the necklace can then be pieced together. Start by arranging the leaves into the order you find most pleasing. There are **4** leaves in the central drop with **3** leaves in both of the outside drops.

21 Bring your thread out of the **top row** of your **base** leaf, take a **second** leaf and *square stitch* it to the first by using the second row of the bead pairs. Pass through he two pairs of beads several times until the two leaves feel secure then fasten off the thread in the usual way.

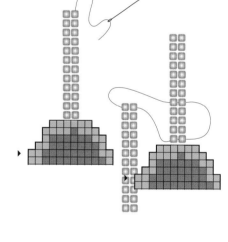

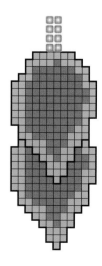

DESIGNER TIP

I find it easiest to work downwards to the tail end of the leaf, then back up and work the top half of the design to finish. The long thin section at the top of the leaf will be used to construct the necklace later.

22 Attach two more leaves in the same way for the central drop and then attach three together for each of the side drops. The long lengths of bead pairs on each of the three leaves at the top are then turned over in a loop and secured to form loops that will fit over the herringbone tube.

23 CONSTRUCTING THE T-BAR AND LOOP:
As you will see from the original necklace I used the same colours for the T-bar and loop that I finished on in the herringbone tube. I thought this added an unusual twist to the finished necklace.

24 WORKING THE T-BAR:
Work a flat piece of even count *peyote* starting with **16 size 11 delica beads** wide x **12** rows. When this is worked, zip the two long ends together to form a tube. Bring the needle in through the **centre** of the tube then pass it out through the **end**. Thread on **1x 4mm crystal** and **1x size 11**. **Miss out** the **size 11** then pass the needle **back through** the **crystal** and out through the other end of the tube. Repeat in exactly the same way securing the second crystal, pass the needle back and forwards several times until the crystals are secure.

25 ADDING THE T-BAR:
Take the end of the herringbone tube and close it up into a ladder as for the other side if you are using the opposite end from the start of the rope. If you wish you can now work a row of *brick stitch* but just adding **4 beads** to **decrease** the opening, the next three rows can contain only **3 beads** decreasing by one once again.

Take the T-bar and attach it to the end of the herringbone tube by working through both the beads on the tube and the T-bar. Finish off in the usual way.

26 ADDING THE LOOP:
Decrease the end of the herringbone tube in exactly the same way as before. Thread on **1x 4mm crystal, 5x size 11s, 1x 4mm, 12x size 11s, 1x 4mm** and **5x size 11s**. Pass the needle **back through** the **first 4mm crystal** to form the loop, then back into the herringbone tube. Pass the needle back around the loops and into the tube several times until the loop seems secure. Finish off in the usual way.

start point ⟶

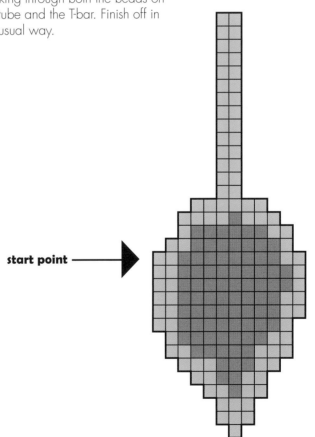

rivolli riots necklace

*This design incorporates **flat circular peyote** as its main technique increasing and decreasing helps to encase the rivolli crystal. Skill level: intermediate*

beads you need

- 14mm rivollis
- 10g size 11 seed beads in 4 colours
- 5g size 15 seed beads in 1 colour
- Beading needle and thread

1 The first section of encasing just uses **two** of the **four size 11 seed beads** and the **size 15 seed beads**.

ROW 1:
Using **1m** thread, pick up **8x size 11 seed beads** in your **first chosen colour**, leaving a **10cm** tail end. Thread back through the beads once again forming a circle. Tie a double knot between the first and last bead to secure.

2 ### ROW 2:
Pass the needle **through** the **first bead** of the 8 once again, pick up **2 size 11 beads** of the **second colour** chosen, these two beads will sit over the **second bead of the first row**. Pass the needle **through** the **third bead** of the first row. Continue until you have added **four 'pairs'** of beads to this second row.

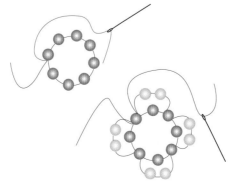

3 ### TO STEP UP:
Pass the needle through the **first bead** of the **first row**, then through the **first 'pair'** of beads added on the **second row**. You will need to **step up** at the end of **every** row.

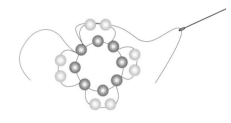

4 ### ROW 3:
Working the colour of the first row, place **1x size 11 seed bead** between each bead of the **second row**, including between each 'pair' of beads.

5 ### ROW 4:
After stepping up, place **2x size 11 seed beads** in the **alternate** colour between each bead of row 3.

6 **ROW 5:**
After stepping up, place **1x size 11 seed bead** in the **alternate** colour between each bead of row 4 including between each 'pair' of beads.

7 **ROW 6:**
After stepping up, place **1x size 11 seed bead** in between each bead of row 5.

8 **ROW 7:**
After stepping up, place **1x size 11 seed bead** in between each bead of row 6.

9 **ROW 8:**
After stepping up, place **1x size 11 seed bead** in between each bead of row 7.

After row 8 has been completed, you can now place the rivolli on top of the beading that has just been completed.

10 **ROW 9:**
After stepping up, place **1x size 15 seed bead** in between each bead of row 8.

11 **ROW 10:**
After stepping up, place **1x size 15 seed bead** in between each bead of row 9. At this point double knot your thread between the last two beads. This will help to hold the tension. If the thread is getting short you can, after threading through two or three more beads, cut off the end of the thread.

DESIGNER TIP
For the last two rows of the initial encasing we are going to use size 15 seed beads. This will really pull the beading in over the top of the rivolli making it feel secure.

12 **TO WORK THE FRILL:**
Secure a new thread on to the bead work, passing through the size 15 seed beads and down through to the second row of size 11 seed beads.

ROW 11:
Work a row of *peyote* using one of the last of the last two colours of **size 11 seed beads**, adding **1 bead** between each bead of the row you are passing the thread through.

Step up through the first bead of the row you have just completed.

13 **ROW 12:**
Add **2x size 11 seed beads** between each bead of row 11. Step up as usual.

14 **ROW 13:**
Add **1x size 11 seed bead** (whichever colour you choose) between each bead of the previous row, including a bead between each 'pair' of beads.

DESIGNER TIP
You have to be really firm on this row to push the beads in between each pair, but this is what makes the beads 'frill'

15 **ROW 14:**
Add **1x size 11 seed bead** (whichever colour you choose) between each bead of the previous row. Your rivolli is now complete.

16 **MAKING UP YOUR RIVOLLIS EARRINGS:**
The finished rivollis can be used as earrings by bringing the needle through one of the outside edge seed beads of the frill, adding **3 seed beads**, passing through the fixing point of a shepherd's crook earring and then picking up **3 more seed beads** before passing back through the seed beads on the frill. Pass the needle back around all the seed beads several times until the earring finding feels secure.

17 **NECKLACE/CHOKER:**
The rivollis can be stitched together by working a small 'bridge' of *peyote stitch* to link each one together. I stitched 3 in a row then added a strap of **peyote stitch 4 beads wide** and turned into a loop by fixing to back of rivolli. A ribbon or suede length can then be threaded through the loop to complete the necklace.

loganberry lariat

necklace

beads you need

FOR THE BERRIES:
- 20g size 8 seed beads
- 10g size 11 seed beads
- beading thread and needle
- stuffing for berries (wool roving)

FOR THE LEAVES:
- 10g size 11 seed beads (green)
- 10g size 11 seed beads (berry mix)

FOR THE SPIRAL ROPE:
- 10g size 11 seed beads (berry mix)
- 30g size 11 seed beads (green)
- Beading thread and needle

*A simple **spiral rope** sets off these juicy fruits, just ripe for picking. Skill level: intermediate/advanced*

1 CREATING THE SPIRAL ROPE:
Pick up **4 core beads** (colour A) and **3 outside edge beads** (colour B). Tie the beads into a circle. Pass the needle back up through the **4A**. Pick up **1A** and **3B*** and let the beads drop down to the work. Pass the needle **up** through the last **3A** and the **A just added**. Pull the thread up firmly. (See **Twist and Shout bracelet** for general instructions for spiral rope.)

2 Place the beads just added so that they sit **next** to the **three** previous outside beads. Pick up **1A** and **3B** and **repeat** from * until you have beaded the required length.

3 CREATING THE LEAVES:

The leaves are worked from the pattern in *square stitch*. It is best to start in the middle of the pattern working downwards then threading back to the centre and working upwards in order to complete the leaf. There are six leaves on each end of the original lariat. Of course, you can add any number you wish. (See the **Fuchsia necklace** for general instructions for *square stitch*.)

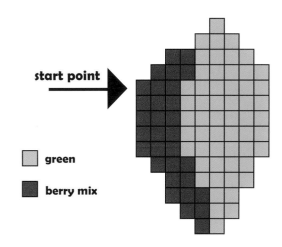

start point

☐ green

■ berry mix

4 CREATING THE LOGANBERRIES:

ROW 1:
Pick up **6 size 11 seed beads**, tie the beads into a circle.

ROW 2:
Work a row of *square stitch* as well as increasing in **two** places by **adding 2 beads** instead of the usual one above the bead of the previous row. **8 beads** in total.

ROW 3:
Work a row of *square stitch* as well as increasing in **two places** once again. **10 beads** in total.

ROW 4:
Work a row of *square stitch* as well as increasing in **two places** once again. **12 beads** in total.

ROW 5:
Work a row of s*quare stitch*, adding **1 size 8 seed bead** to **each bead** of the previous row.

ROW 6:
Work a row of *square stitch* adding **1 size 8 seed bead** as in row 5.

ROW 7:
Work a row of *square stitch* adding **1 size 8 seed bead** as in row 6.

ROW 8:
We now need to decrease back down to form the shape of the fruit by working a row of *square stitch* but you will need to decrease by **2 size 8 seed beads.**

ROW 9:
Work a row of *square stitch* in size 8 seed bead decreasing by **2 beads** once again.

ROW 10:
Work a row of *square stitch* in size 8 seed beads decreasing a further **2 beads.**

ROW 11:
Work a row of *square stitch* in size 8 decreasing again by **two** beads. **Note:** It is at this point that you could start to stuff your berry if you wish. This is done by using lots of small pieces so that you can really stuff the bottom narrow point of the fruit.

ROW 12:
Work a row of *square stitch* using **size 11 seed beads** and **no decreasing** on this row.

ROW 13:
Work a row of *square stitch*, using size 11s but this time **decreasing** by **two beads.**

ROW 14:
Finally, **add 1 bead** at the base of the loganberry to finish.

For increasing and decreasing please refer to p59/60, Monets poppy necklace.

5 LARIAT CONSTRUCTION:

Three loganberries are added to each end of the spiral rope. The leaves are attached with two or three seed beads worked into the spiral rope.

DESIGNER TIP

When each row is completed, remember to thread the needle back through the beads just added to secure as you would with flat square stitch!

cuffed to bits bracelet

bracelet

The mixture of pearls and seed beads creates an interesting textured effect. Skill level: intermediate

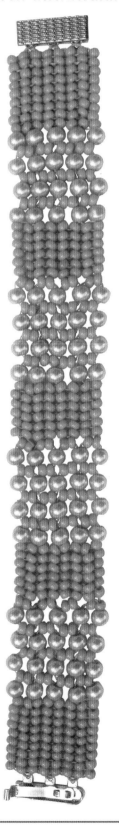

beads you need
- 10-15g size 8 seed beads
- 80-100 4mm pearls
- Bar clasp with 3 fixing points
- KO beading thread
- Beading needle

1 ROW 1:
Thread the needle with **1m** beading thread. Thread on **2x size 8** seed beads to within **20cm** from the tail end. Pass the needle back through the first bead added and pull up on the thread so that the beads sit side by side.

2 Pass the needle **down** through the **second bead** added, pick up a third bead, pass the needle back **down** through the **second bead** once again then **up** through the **third bead** just added. Continue adding beads in the same way until you have added **all 8** initial beads to the ladder. If the ladder feels a little on the loose side, you can always thread back through the beads to tighten it up.

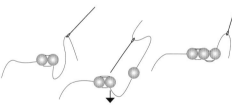

3 STARTING TO HERRINGBONE: ROW 2:
Hold the ladder base with the working thread on the top side of the ladder and the end of the thread hanging downwards. Pick up **2x size 8** beads. Pass the needle down through the next bead along. Give the two beads a light tap so that they sit fairly flat on top of the base size 8 beads. Pass the needle up through the **third size 8 bead** along the ladder. Pick up **2** further **size 8s** and pass the needle **down** through the **next** size 8 along. Continue working in the same way until you reach the end of the ladder.

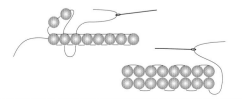

4 TO STEP UP:
Turn your beadwork around so that the end thread is hanging back at the beginning. Pass the needle **back up** through the ladder bead next to the end bead. Then pass the needle **up** through the **first** bead on the **second** row.

5 ROW 3:
Pick up **two** beads, pass the needle **down** through the next bead along. Then pass the needle up through the **first bead** of the **second pair** along. Continue along in the same way for the rest of the row.

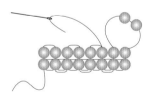

The first section of the bracelet contains **nine rows** of herringbone.

6 RIGHT ANGLE WEAVE PEARL ROWS:
Bring the needle **up** through the **first bead** on the **end** of the last row. Pick up **1x 4mm pearl**, **2x size 7** and **1x 4mm**, pass the needle **down** through the next **size 8** of the herringbone row.

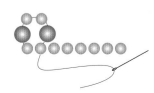

7 Pass the needle **up** through the third size 8 seed bead and the **pearl** just added. Pick up **2x size 8s** and **1x 4mm pearl**. Pass the needle **down** through the **fourth** bead along on the *herringbone* row. Continue in the same manner until the row is complete. There should be **five pearls** in total sitting on this first row of *right angle weave*.

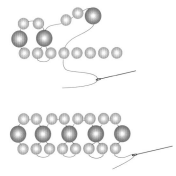

8 **TO STEP UP TO THE NEXT ROW:**
Pass the needle **back up** through the **second size 8 bead**, then up through the **last pearl**, then along the last **two seed beads** added. Pick up **1x 4mm pearl, 2x size 8 seed beads** and **1x 4mm pearl**, pass the needle back through the **two seed beads** forming a circle, then **back up** through the side pearl.

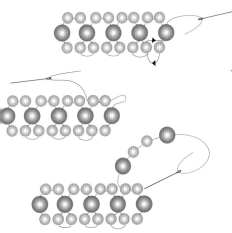

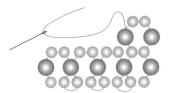

9 Pick up **2x seed beads** and **1x 4mm pearl**, pass the needle through the next **2 seed beads** along, through the **pearl**, through the **2x seed beads** just added and **down** through the **pearl** and across through the **next 2 seed beads** of the **previous** row.

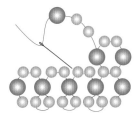

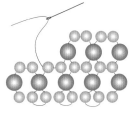

Continue in the same manner until the row is complete.

10 There are **four** rows of *right angle weave*. When these are complete you need to revert back to *herringbone*. This is very simple to do, work your way around the beads until your needle and thread are coming out of the **first bead** of the **second pair** on the last row. Continue to **add pairs** which then puts you back into *herringbone stitch*.

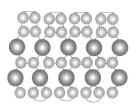

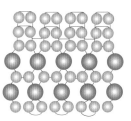

11 **BRACELET LENGTH:**
The original bracelet has **9 rows** of *herringbone* at each end of the bracelet and **3 sections of 7 rows** divided by **4 sections of 4-row** *right angle weave* pearl sections. Of course, these can be altered in length to fit you. If you start with the middle sections of the bracelet you can lengthen or shorten the two end sections to fit.

12 **ADDING THE CLASP:**
Pass the needle **up** through the **second bead** along on the **base row** of the ladder at one end of the bracelet. Pass through the end fixing point of the clasp and **down** through the **next size 8** along. Bring back around these beads again two or three times until things seem secure. Repeat until all three fixing points are secure. Repeat on the other side in the same way.

deco delight necklace

An Egyptian-style collar, given a modern twist. Try different colour combinations.
Skill level: beginner

beads you need

- 20g 4mm cube beads
- 20g size 5 triangles
- 10g size 6 seed beads
- 20g size 8 seed beads
- 5g size 10 triangles
- 2-bar clasp
- Beading thread and needle

3 Thread on **2 more triangles**, pass the needle **down** through the next cube then back **up** through the next cube as before.

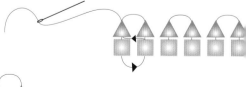

Continue adding **size 5 triangles** in the same way until you reach the end of the row.

1 Thread the beading needle with **1m** beading thread. Using the **4mm cubes** thread on **2 cubes** and move them down to within **15cm** of the tail end of the thread.

The 2 beads will then click together, side by side. Go back through the second cube and then first and second cube once more to secure.

2 Continue to add **one cube** at a time until you have added **54 cubes** in total.

Herringbone stitch will now be used to add the four further rows that make up the widest part of the necklace.

Bring the needle **up** through the **last cube** added, thread on **2x size 5 triangles** and pass the needle **down** through the **next cube** along, then **up** through the **third cube** along.

4 **ROW 3:**
Bring the needle **up** through the **penultimate bead (no.2)** of the **first** row and then **diagonally up** through the **last** bead of the row of beads just added. Make sure that the thread lies snugly under the beads and has not got caught up anywhere.

5 Row 3 is worked in **size 6 seed beads**. Thread on **2x size 6 seed beads**. Pass the needle **down** through the **size 5 triangle** next to the one the thread is coming out of and then pass the needle **up** through the **first triangle** of the **next pair** along. Thread on **2x size 6 seed beads** and pass the needle **down** through the **next triangle** along.

Continue to add **size 6 seed beads** in pairs until the third row is complete.

6 ROW 4:
Add a further row of **size 5 triangles**.

7 ROW 5:
When you work this final row, thread on **1x size 8 seed bead**, **1x size 10 triangle** and **1x size 8 seed bead**. These are the beads added on to the pairs of **size 5 triangles** added in **row 4**.

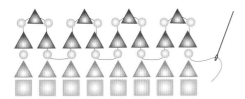

8 To finish this central section, a small *picot edge* is added on the other side of this central section of the necklace. Pass the needle **through** the **end cube** of your beading on the opposite side you were working on.

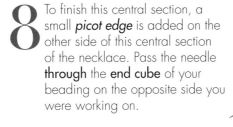

9 Thread on **1x size 8 seed bead**, **1x size 10 triangle** and **1x size 8 seed bead**. Pass the needle **down** through the **next cube** along and **up** through the **third cube**, add on the next 'set' of beads, keep adding edging until you run out of cubes.

You have now completed the central section of your necklace.

10 TO FINISH:
You need to add enough cubes to each side of the central section to fit your neck correctly. This is done in exactly the same way as before.

DESIGNER TIP

You must have an even number of cubes in order to add the picot to the whole of the necklace.

11 THE FIRST STEP DOWN
contains **2x size 5 triangles**, **2x size 6 seed beads**, **1x size 8 seed bead**, **1x size 10 triangle** and **1x size 8 seed bead**.

12 THE SECOND STEP DOWN
contains **2x size 5 triangles**, **1x size 8 seed bead**, **1x size 10 triangle** and **1x size 8 seed bead**, this then leads nicely down to the small continual *picot*.

13 Work the *picot* again along the top edge of the necklace so that it meets with the central section picot.

When you have joined the *picots* together you can thread through and add the bottom section to match. To step the design I created **two** *herringbone* loops to lead the eye down to the final *picot*.

14 ATTACHING THE CLASP:
When the ladder of cubes is long enough, bring the needle out of either end of the final cube. Pass the needle through the fixing point of the 2-bar clasp then back into the cube. Thread and pass the needle through the other fixing point of the clasp. Repeat this movement several times until the clasp feels secure.

steam punk chain

necklace

beads you need

SPIRAL ROPE:
- 10g size 11 seed beads (core)
- 30g size 11 seed beads (spiral)

MATERIALS: OUTER EMBELLISHMENT
- 10g size 11 seed beads
- 30g size 5 triangles
- 30g size 8 triangles
- 20g 4mm cube beads
- Beading thread and needles
- Toggle or clasp of your choice
- Pendant or large bead of your choice

This chain would complement any large pendant.
Skill level: beginner

1 The base of the chain is constructed in spiral rope. Using **1m** of beading thread, pick up **4x core beads** and **3x outside spiral beads**.

2 Pass the needle back up through the **4 core beads** once again.

3 Holding the beads in your hand, push the **3 outside beads** over to the **left hand side**.

4 *Thread on **1x core** and **3x outside beads**, let the beads drop down to the beadwork.

5 Pass the needle **through** the last **3 core beads** added and the **last core bead** just added, pull the thread firmly.

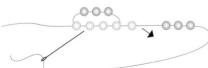

6 Position the outside beads just added until they sit **right next to** the three previously placed outside beads.

Pick up **1x core** and **3x outside beads** and **repeat from *** until you have the length you require.

7 OUTER EMBELLISHMENT: Making sure you have a good length of thread and passing the needle **down** through the **first set of 3 outside beads**. Pick up **2x size 11 seed beads**, **1x size 8 triangle** and **2x size 11 seed beads**.

8 Pass the needle **down** through the same set of **three beads** but in the **opposite** direction.

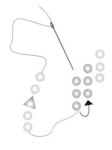

9 Pass the needle **up** through the next set of three outside beads and pick up **2x size 11 seed beads**, **1x size 5 triangle** and **2x size 11 seed beads**, pass the needle **back up** through the second set of three beads.

8 —

— 5

10 Pass the needle **down** through the third set of three beads, pick up **2x size 11 seed beads**, **1x 4mm cube** and **2x size 11 beads**, pass the needle **back down** through the **third set of beads** and up through the **fourth set of three beads** on the initial spiral.

11 Continue adding loops in the same manner, the next central bead will be a **size 5 triangle**, then a **size 8 triangle**.

The correct order of the central beads are: **size 8 triangle, size 5 triangle, 4mm cube, size 5 triangle, size 8 triangle, size 5 triangle, 4mm cube, size 5 triangle, size 8 triangle** and so on and so on…

12 TO FINISH: Of course many different combinations can be tried to achieve different effects. I have made two identical lengths of chain and placed my chosen pendant in the centre joining the two pieces together through the pendant until secure

Lastly, add a toggle or clasp or your choice.

crystal cascade necklace

beads you need

- 16-20 large crystals
- 75-95 small crystals
- Size 11 seed beads
- Toggle clasp
- Beading needle and thread

This necklace will showcase any crystals – try using other shapes for a different look.
Skill level: beginner

1 Thread a beading needle with **1.5m** beading thread. Using a double knot and leaving a **15cm** end, secure the thread to one end of the toggle clasp using the fixing point.

2 Thread on **30x size 11** seed beads.

3 Pick up **1 large crystal** followed by **10x seed beads**, repeat the sequence until the necklace is long enough, bearing in mind that you still need to add **30 size 11 seed beads** and the other end of the clasp.

4 Add **30 seed beads**, pass the needle through the fixing point on the other end of the toggle clasp and pass the needle **back down through** the **30 size 11 seed beads** and then work a **double knot** between the **thirtieth** seed bead and the **first** large crystal.

5 **ADDING THE DROPS:**
Pass the needle through the **first** crystal and the **first** of the 10 seed beads. Pick up **3 seed beads**, **1x small crystal** and **1x seed bead**. Missing out the seed bead, pass the needle **back** through the **crystal** and the **3 seed beads**. Next, pass the needle **through** the next **2 seed beads** along on the original row.

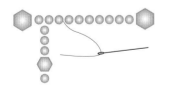

6 Pick up **7x seed beads**, **1x crystal** and **1x seed bead**, missing out the last seed bead, thread the needle **back up** through the **crystal** and **7x seed beads**. Pass the needle through the **next 2 seed beads** on the original row.

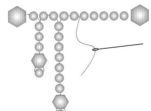

7 The next drop contains **9x seed beads**, then thread through the next **2 seed beads**, then a drop with **7x seed beads** once again, finishing with a drop of **3x seed beads**, passing through the **last seed bead** then through the next large **crystal** and the **first** of the next 10 seed beads before repeating the five drops once again.

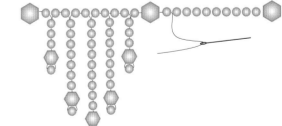

8 Repeat in the same way until the drops are complete. Pass the needle through the last **30 seed beads**, up and around the **toggle clasp**, before **double knotting** between **two beads**, threading through a couple more beads and cutting off any excess thread to finish.

9 Lastly, re-thread the other tail end, pass it through a further few beads, double knot once again between two beads, thread through a couple more beads before cutting off any excess thread.

monet's poppy necklace

necklace

beads you need

- Delica beads: DB 295 (1);
  DB 723 (2); DB 602 (3);
  DB 654 (4); DB 004; DB 310
- Long and short beading needles
- KO/Nymo beading thread
- Beading needle
- Note pad, pencil and rubber
  (to mark your chart off)
- Toggle clasp

Three petals are added on top of the design creating a layered effect.
Skill level: intermediate/ advanced

1 Firstly, empty a small amount of all **six colours** to be used on to your beading mat. Thread a beading needle with **1m** beading thread.

2 STARTING TO SQUARE STITCH:
Place the poppy pattern next to you and note the starting arrow on the grid, then working from the left to right, thread on the first colour bead down to about **10cm** from the tail end of the thread. Pass the needle back up through the bead creating a 'stop' bead.

3 Continue to thread on this entire first row of beads, there should be **38 beads** in total including the 'stop' bead.

4 Thread the **first** bead of the **second row** on to your thread and position the bead so that it sits directly **underneath** the last right hand bead of the **first** row.

5 Pass the needle back through the **last bead** of the **first row**, then turn the needle passing **back through** the **first bead** of the **second row** just added.

6 Continue along the row adding beads in exactly the same way, being careful to note the colour changes as you work.

7 When the second row is complete, pass the needle back through the initial row of beads added, then thread through the second row once again.

8 Threading through the two rows of beads gives extra stability to the beads and bring them nicely into line.

Continue to add rows in the same manner until you reach the point at which the poppy petals overlap the outer edge of the necklace.

9 **SQUARE STITCH – INCREASING ON THE OUTSIDE EDGES:**
To increase on either of the outside edges, bring the needle through the last bead on the row you wish to increase. Thread on one more bead, plus the first bead of the next row.

Thread back through the increase bead.

10 Thread through the first bead of the next row and continue along in the usual way, You can add as many beads as you wish for an increase, just *square stitch* your way back into the main section of the beadwork to secure.

monet's poppy necklace

necklace

11 **SQUARE STITCH – DECREASING ON THE OUTSIDE EDGES:**
When the previous row is finished prior to the decreasing row, run the threads through as usual. Firstly through the row above them and then through the row you have just completed. However, instead of running the thread through the entire row bring the needle out of the bead you wish to start the next decreased row.

12 Thread on a bead and go back through the bead the thread is coming out of, then go back through the bead just added.

13 Continue along the row until you reach the bead where you wish to start the next row. Add the first bead of the next row and continue as usual.

14 **CONSTRUCTING THE POPPY:**
The poppy has three extra petals that need to be worked separately, then *stab-stitched* into place sitting over the original corresponding petal.

15 Work the three petals in the colours stated by the number key using the starting point pointed to on the chart. Work down at first to the bottom tip of the petal then, turn and work up the other way to the top of the petal to finish.

16 When all three are complete, *stab-stitch* each petal into place by making four tiny stitches in each corner of the petals.

17 **THE CENTRE OF THE POPPY:**
Working just in the centre of the poppy on top of the **004 beads**, work tiny loops of **three beads** over that entire area to give texture to the centre.

18 To string the necklace, attach a fresh piece of thread to one side of the poppy where the necklace join is indicated on the chart. String on as many black delica beads as you need for the correct length of your neck. Take one half of your clasp and pass the needle through the fixing point, threading back down through the last two beads added.

19 The loops are then added by picking up **ten 004 beads (purple iris)**, pass the needle back down through the first bead just threaded on to create the loop, pass the needle through the next bead along on the original necklace row.

Continue to add loops between each bead on the original row. These loops get smaller as you work to the end of the necklace.

20 **ADDING THE RED FLASHES:**
The red sections of loops can be added at any point along the original row. They are made up of **9 loops** and can be any combination of reds or amounts of beads.

21 Use a variety of your reds to do this and add as many red sections as you like. When the first half of the necklace is complete repeat in exactly the same way for the other side attaching the other half of the clasp.

Lastly, add a few loops along the top of the poppy as indicated on the diagram below.

POPPY PATTERN

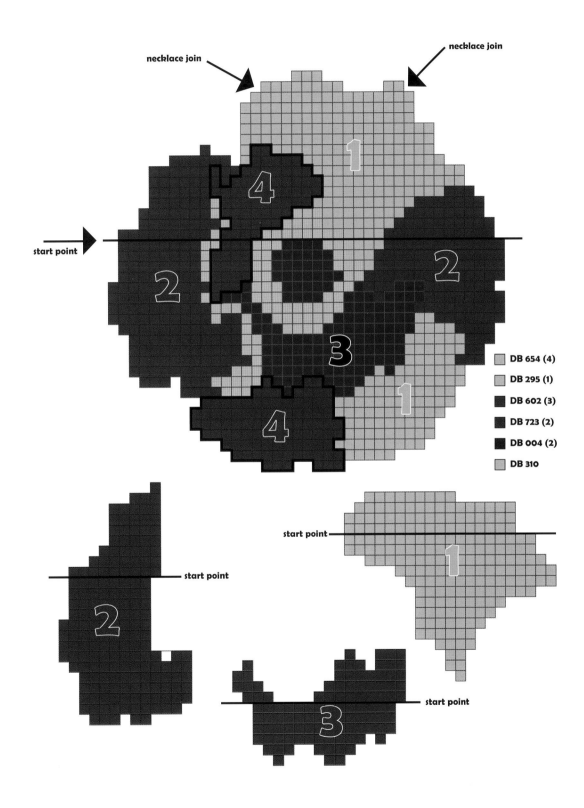

necklace join

necklace join

start point

1

4

2

2

3

1

4

DB 654 (4)
DB 295 (1)
DB 602 (3)
DB 723 (2)
DB 004 (2)
DB 310

start point

2

start point

1

start point

3

art nouveau crystals necklace

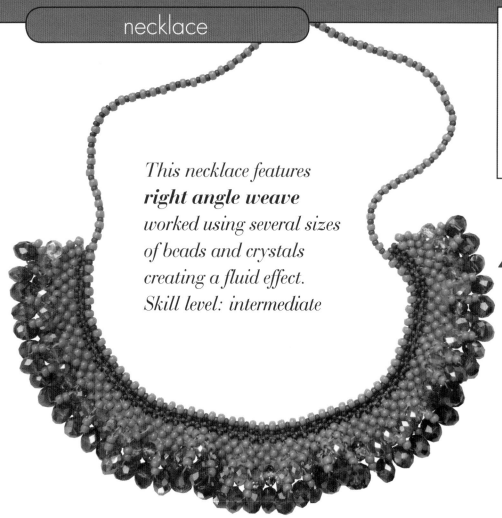

This necklace features **right angle weave** *worked using several sizes of beads and crystals creating a fluid effect.*
Skill level: intermediate

beads you need

- 30g size 8 seed beads
- 10g size 11 seed beads
- 53x 4x6mm cushion crystals
- 53x 6x8mm cushion crystals
- S-lon or fireline beading thread and needle
- Toggle clasp or bead and loop fastener

1 Starting with **size 8 seed beads**, pick up **4x beads** and tie them into a ring. Pass the needle through beads **1** and **2**. Pick up beads **5**, **6** and **7**; pass the needle back **through** the **second** bead.

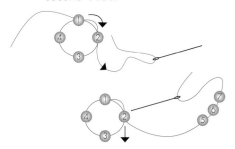

2 Pass the needle back through beads **5** and **6**, pick up **3** more **seed beads** and repeat until you have **54** completed right angle circles in this initial row.

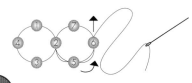

3 ROW 2:
To start the **second row**, pass the needle through the bottom bead of the last completed circle of the initial row. Pick up **1x size 8 seed bead**, **1x 4x6mm crystal** and **1x size 8 seed bead**.

Pass the needle **back through** the **bottom** bead of the initial row, through the **size 8 seed bead**, **4x6mm crystal**, **size 8 seed bead**; pass the needle through the next bottom bead of the initial row. Continue in this way until you reach the other end of the initial row.

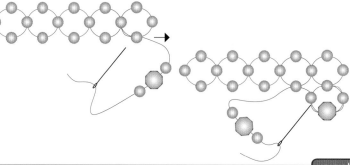

4 ROW 3:
Pass the needle **through** the **first** set of **crystal** *right angle weave* and continue around until the needle is passing through the **second crystal** in from the edge (this is to stop the bigger crystal sticking out of each end of the necklace) of row 2. Pick up **2x size 8 seed beads**, **1x 6x8mm crystal** and **2x size 8 seed beads**, pass the needle **back** through the crystal of the previous row.

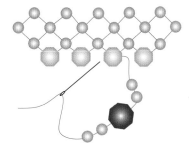

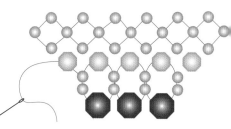

5

Pass the needle back through the **2x size 8 seed beads**, the **crystal** and **2x size 8 seed beads**. Pass the needle through the **next crystal** along before picking up **2x size 8 seed beads** and **1x crystal**. Continue adding beads until the end of the row.

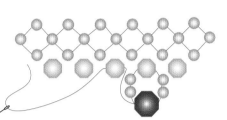

6

ROW 4:
This row is actually worked **above** row 1; work a row of *right angle weave* in **size 11 seed beads**.

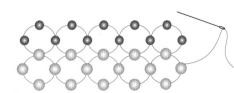

7

ROW 5:
Work a **second** row of *right angle weave* in **size 11 seed beads** on top of **row 4**.

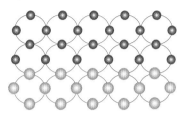

8

ROW 6:
Work a row of *peyote stitch* using size 8 seed beads.

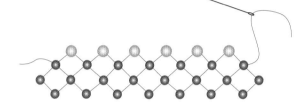

9

To complete the necklace, pass a thread through the complete central length of the necklace, taking in both the **size 11** and **size 8 seed bead** to give added strength to the 'heavy' central section of the necklace. Pass the needle out through the last **size 11 seed bead**, then start to add **1x size 8 seed bead**, **1x size 11 seed bead** alternately until you have a long enough length for one side of the necklace.

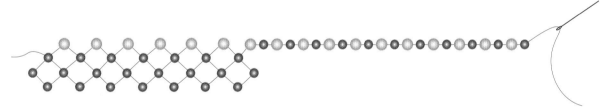

10

BEAD AND LOOP FASTENER:
Finally add **2** more **size 11 seed beads**, **1x 6x8mm crystal** and **3 size 11 seed beads**, missing out the final **3 seed beads**. Pass the needle back down the entire length just added, when you reach the main body of the necklace, wind your needle around the beads following the pattern until you are able to turn and pass the needle back through the length just completed to strengthen it.

11

To create the loop side of the fastener, add beads to the other end of the necklace, then thread on **20x size 11 seed beads**, pass the needle **back through** the **first added** to form a loop, then pass the needle back down the length of newly added beads, repeat again as before to strengthen.

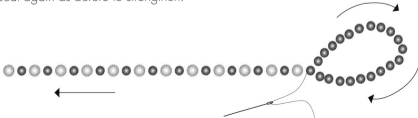

inspirational pinks necklace

beads you need

- Selection medium size focal beads
- Selection of pearls (any size)
- Selection random crystals
- 10g 2x size 11 seed beads
- 10g size 6 seed beads
- Beading needle and thread

This necklace is perfect for all those 'one-off' beads you have treasured but have no idea where to use them. Skill level: beginner

1 The idea of this necklace is to use the focal beads in a random way, so don't worry too much about what order you use them in. You will notice that **a size 6 seed bead** is used on both sides of the focal bead since many focal beads have a large hole and size 11 beads will slip through the holes.

2 The initial row is worked by threading on **20x size 11 seed beads, 1x size 6 seed bead, 1x focal bead** and **1x size 6 seed bead**. Repeat in the same order until the necklace reaches the desired length.

3 **Two further rows** are worked just adding **seed beads, pearls and crystals**, with just enough **seed beads** in between to stretch across to the next focal bead. These lines of beads can also be wound in and out of each other for extra effect. Do remember to pass through the **size 6** either side as well as the **focal bead** – this gives extra stability. Double knot your thread to finish.

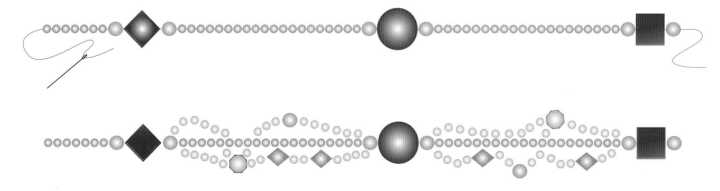

www.thebeadscene.com

beads you need

- 7x feature flowers
- 287 4mm pink pearls
- 448 green pearls
- Beading needle and thread

1 The flowers are decorated first before the design is strung together. Using **1m thread**, pick up **9x pink pearls**, pass the needle through the centre of the flower and **back through** the **9 pearls**. Secure in place by double knotting the end and working thread.

This necklace could be made in smaller proportions if desired by using smaller flower shapes.
Skill level: beginner

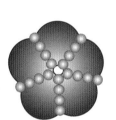

2 Continue in the same way only using **8x pink pearls** for the other **4 loops of pink pearls** in between each petal. Work each flower in the same way until all are decorated.

3 JOINING THE FLOWERS TOGETHER:
Pass the needle out through the **fourth pink pearl** on any one of the loops. Thread on **35x 4mm green pearls**. Pass the needle through a corresponding **pink pearl** on another completed flower.

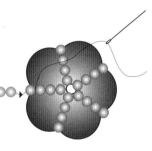

4 Pick up **2x green pearls**, pass the needle through the **third bead** along on the initial row of green pearls. Pick up **5x green pearls**, pass the needle through the **eighth green pearl** of the initial row.

5 Keep picking up **5x green beads**, **missing 5** on the original row and passing through the **sixth bead along** until you reach the other flower where you will need to add **2x beads** as at the start of this section to complete. It is a good idea to pass up and down the lacing two or three times to add extra security.

6 The lacing is worked in exactly the same way until all the flowers are connected. You will notice that because the flowers have 5 loops they do hang a little off centre. I feel this adds to the boho look – or at least that's my excuse!

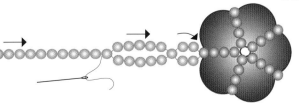

DESIGNER TIP

If you feel the loops on the flowers are too loose, pass the needle and thread back through all the pearls again until the work feeds secure.